Tapestry & Needlepoint

Marshall Cavendish London & New York

Title page: Part of the Hastings Embroidery. It was commissioned by the Borough of Hastings from the Royal School of Needlework, to celebrate the 900th anniversary of the Battle of Hastings. A team of 18 embroiderers took just over a year to finish the completed embroidery which consists of 27 panels, each measuring nine feet by three feet, 243 feet in all.

Edited by Gabrielle Weaver

Published by Marshall Cavendish Publications Limited, 58 Old Compton Street, London W1V 5PA

ISBN 0 85685 187 6

Printed in Great Britain

Introduction

Tapestry and Needlepoint are two of the most beautiful traditional crafts to be enjoying an exciting new revival. Both have had many devoted followers for some years, but at last manufacturers of yarns and threads have produced lovely new colors and textures and many designers have brought their original designs right up to date.

Now with this book, anyone new to these crafts will find everything that they will need to know to produce the lovely designs we include, and to create stunning original designs of their own.

We tell you how to build a small frame loom for your tapestry weaving, and our introduction to tapestry is a comprehensive sampler which includes every shape, pattern and design feature you could need to weave more complex pieces.

We also tell you how to choose the right yarns and colors for canvaswork, how to choose and prepare your canvas, work it and finish it, all the techniques for tracing patterns, working in a frame and using the varied textures of the stitches for maximum coverage and interest.

All the patterns and designs are fully illustrated in color with careful instructions, color guides, charts and material requirements. The basic stitch library will teach you all the stitches if you are new to needlepoint and refresh your memory if you are already an expert. The many patterns for cushions, lighter and glasses cases, hand-made personalized gifts, stool tops, picture frames, belts, bags and buckles provide the ideal practice ground for using all the traditional skills, while taking full advantage of all the lovely yarns, colors and textures available today.

Suppliers
To order Anchor Tapisserie Wool
by mail write to:
Yarns Galore,
2422 Ponce de Leon Boulevard,
Coral Cables, Florida 33164
For your nearest supplier of
D.M.C. yarn write to:
The D.M.C. Company,
107 Trumbull Street,
Elizabeth, New Jersey 07206
For purse frames write to:
The Jacmore Company,
36 West 25th Street,
New York, N.Y. 10010
and include a sketch and
measurements of the frame size
desired.

Photographers
Malcolm Aird 36, 53
Camera Press 70, 80
John Carter 82
Roger Charity 56/7, 78
Alan Duns 51
Fabbri 25, 26, 29
Barbara Firth 32, 37, 42/3, 72–75
I. Hollowood 54/55
Chris Lewis 50–61, 68
Rob Matheson 22, 23
Dick Miller 12, 18, 19, 21
Roger Philips 76/77
Renee Robinson 28
Johnny Ryan 17, 20, 21, 22
Joy Simpson 48
Transworld 11
Jerry Tubby 8, 10, 13, 14, 15, 23
Peter Watkins 26

Designers
J. & P. Coats Ltd. 56/7, 82
DMC 86
Sue Gamson 68, 76, 77
David Hill 8–23
Leila Kerr 61
Susan Money 64, 65
By permission of Louis J. Gartner Jnr.
& William Morrow & Co. Inc.,
from Needlepoint Designs 40, 41
Mary Rhodes & Eileen Lowcock 49, 50
Mrs. J. M. Stuart 53

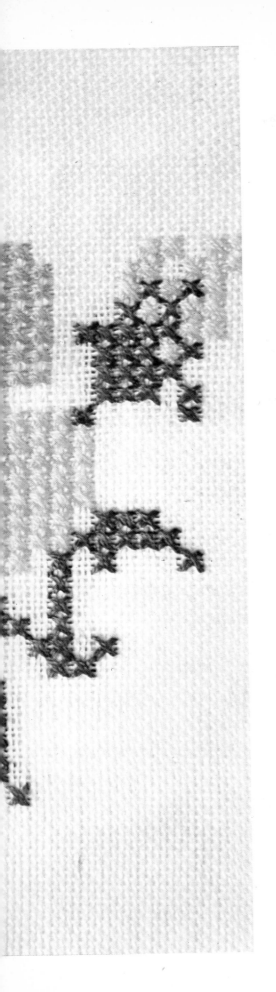

Contents

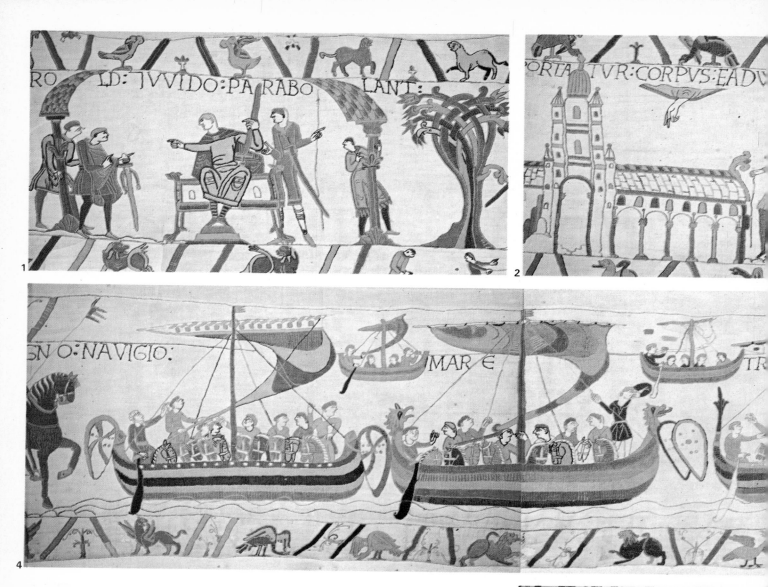

Introduction to Tapestry

The famous Bayeux Tapestry is no less than 231 feet long and 20 inches wide. It consists of seventy-two scenes, depicting the Norman Conquest of England in the eleventh century. It is beautiful and invaluable as a record of early English history, and early English art, but strangely enough it is not a tapestry. It is in fact, an example of early embroidery, worked in wools on a linen fabric, but someone called it a tapestry and the name has never been changed.

It is interesting to compare the famous work with examples of real tapestry. Genuine tapestry is in fact a technique of weaving, on a small loom, in small sections which are then stitched together. The pictures and patterns are woven into cloth.

In earlier times this technique was used to produce carpets and wall hangings, which, besides providing a record of events and being a means of decorating walls and cold stone floors, were ingenious and hard wearing draft excluders.

Both tapestry and embroidery on canvas are now enjoying an understandable revival and continue to provide the limitless pleasure of time-honored needlecrafts to the many devotees who have filled their leisure hours with practicing and keeping the traditional skills alive.

1. In 1064 Harold takes a message from Edward the Confessor to William naming him as successor to the English throne.

2. Edward the Confessor dies, having just recommended Harold as his successor. His body is taken to be buried in Westminster Abbey.

3. Harold breaks his oath to William and is crowned king instead. On hearing the news, William calls his men to prepare for war.

4. With men and horses on board, the Norman vessels set sail.

5. The Norman army lands at Pevensey. Meanwhile, Harold is fighting the Norwegians in the North; he does not hear of William's landing until four days later, and, collecting what levies he can, makes a forced march south.

6. The Battle of Hastings; with their bows and arrows and heavy war-horses, the Normans have a decisive advantage over the defenders. Here their cavalry charge the tattered and exhausted English ranks.

7. Harold plucks the fatal arrow from his eye.

Tapestry frame loom

The deceptively simple frame loom is much used by professional weavers of tapestry and sculptural weaving. The advantage of a frame, whether small or large, is that it is cheap and simple to construct, simple to set up and operate and gives great freedom in the variety of materials and shapes that can be woven.

More sophisticated looms were developed simply to fulfill the need for quicker and greater production of lengths of cloth. Essentially the frame loom is used for creating an individual piece of weaving, whereby each separate colored shape is woven and joined together to build up a complete picture or design. The great advantage of the frame loom is that it offers scope for endless variation and experiment with texture, color and materials, so that the process of weaving is an exciting end in itself.

To make the frame
2 feet by 3 feet 6 inches
You will need

- [ ] Two pieces of pinewood 3 feet 6 inches by 2 inches by 1 inch thick.
- [ ] Four pieces of pinewood 2 feet by 2 inches by 1 inch thick.
- [ ] Two blocks of pinewood 2 inches by 1 inch by 3 inches.
- [ ] Two pieces of pinewood $\frac{1}{4}$ inch by $\frac{3}{4}$ inch by 28 inches long, for cross sticks.
- [ ] $1\frac{1}{2}$ inch screws.
- [ ] $1\frac{1}{4}$ inch finishing nails.
- [ ] Warp cotton or heavy crochet cotton.

Put frame together as in fig.1, using two screws per corner on each side of the frame. On one side the screws should be placed at top left and bottom right, and on the reverse of the frame at top right and bottom left. This is to prevent the screws coinciding.

In the center, between the cross pieces at the top and bottom, insert the small blocks and screw in position. These act as spacers to prevent bending under the warp tension (fig.2).

Starting 2 inches from one inside edge of the frame, mark off cross pieces A and B (fig.3) into $\frac{1}{2}$ inch intervals (making 33 along each edge), and knock small nails or $1\frac{1}{4}$ inch finishing nails into the cross pieces on the marks at an angle (fig.4). The top and bottom pins should be exactly in line with each other.

Stagger the nails, as this helps to prevent the wood splitting and stops you catching your fingers between the nails when putting on the warp (fig.3).

Although frames such as picture frames may be used, they are not usually strong enough to withstand the tension from the warp without some sort of modification. As frames are so simple to construct, it is better to build one for the purpose than to make do with something you may have lying around.

The frame loom, when completed, measures 2 feet by 3 feet 6 inches. Although a smaller frame than this can be used, it would severely limit the size of any weaving, as you have to allow 4 inches in the width and 9 inches in

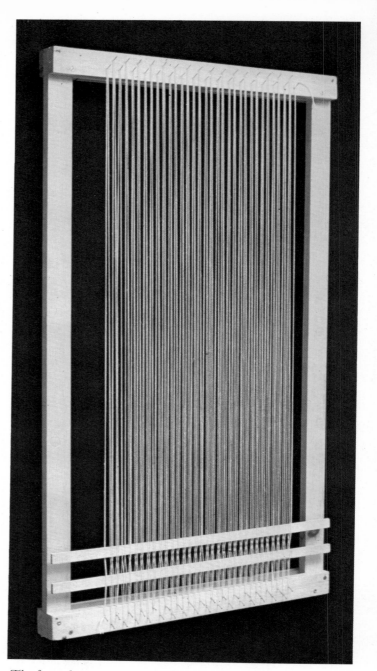

The frame loom warped up ready for weaving the tapestry sampler.

the length for wastage. The tapestry sampler needs to be woven on a frame this size, if you wish to follow the design instructions exactly as we give them. However, if you do make a smaller frame and wish to produce the sampler reduced, it is essential that you scale down all the measurements exactly or the finished product will be unbalanced. Do not be daunted by the prospect; with the aid of some graph paper it is relatively simple and you can make the sampler, or a design of your own, for a specific purpose, such as a cushion cover, bag, small framed picture or hanging. We advise a beginner, however, to start with this design because it incorporates all the features of basic tapestry weaving, such as delineation of color and texture, how to weave circles, diagonal and vertical designs, joining sections of a design, as well as the basic techniques of manipulating the bobbins, starting and finishing quantities of yarn, etc. But just as size is not really a limiting factor, there

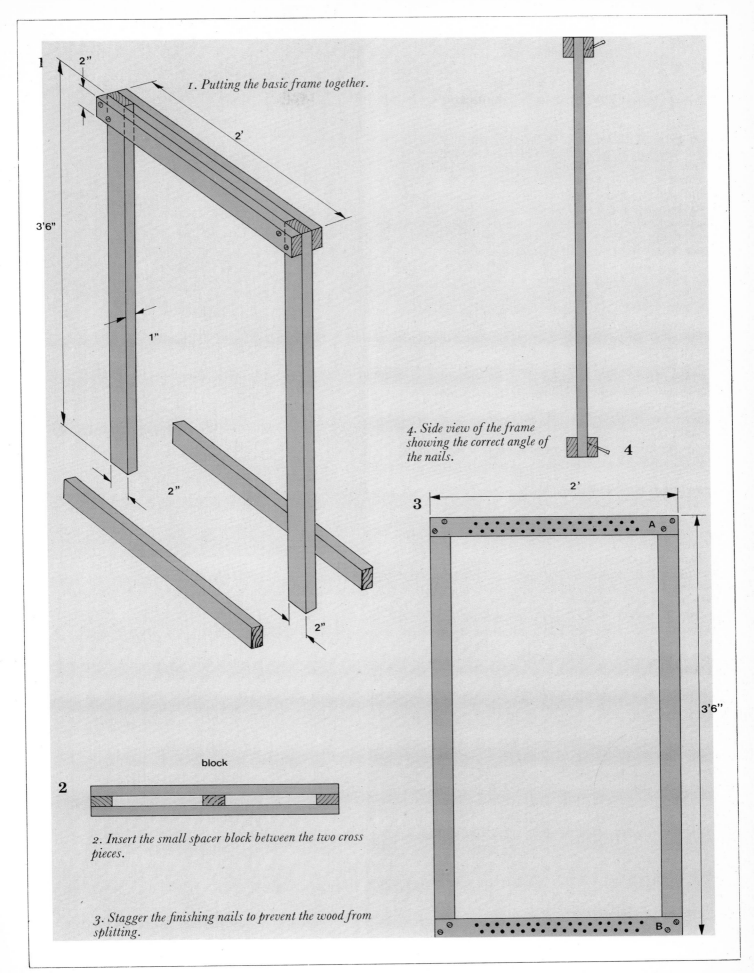

1. Putting the basic frame together.

2'

2"

3'6"

1"

2"

2"

block

2

2. Insert the small spacer block between the two cross pieces.

3. Stagger the finishing nails to prevent the wood from splitting.

4. Side view of the frame showing the correct angle of the nails.

4

3

2'

A

B

3'6"

9

is no reason why you must produce your sampler in the colors given. We have used black and white for clarity.

Place the frame on a table or chair and lean it against a wall. It may be helpful to lay the loom on its side as warping (putting on the warp threads) is usually easier from side to side rather than up and down.

The following instructions are for putting the warp on the frame while it is on its side.

Wind half of your spool of cotton twine either onto an empty spool or into a ball. Take the thread from each spool and use them together as a double thread.

Tie the cotton warp thread to the first nail at the top of the frame on the left hand side (fig.5).

Holding the threads reasonably tightly, carry them across to the right hand side.

Pass them around first nail at the top on the right hand side.

Carry them to the second nail on the left.

Loop the threads around the left nail and carry them over to the second nail on the right.

Now carry the threads over to the third nail on the right.

Continue this process downward, looping the threads around each nail and maintaining the same tension on the warp threads.

When you come to the last nail, secure with a temporary knot. The two extra threads at the beginning and end are worked together to form the selvedges.

Sett

You now have a sett of eight ends per inch (fig.6). In tapestry the average spacing between the warp ends is between four and twelve ends per inch.

Correcting the tension

Invariably, there is an unevenness in the tension of the warp after you have finished and this can be corrected. It is worth taking the trouble to get an even tension over the warp to prevent difficulties occurring when weaving. The tension can be corrected by working the slack along the warp from the tight side to the loose side. This is done by pulling on each warp end on the side of the nail which is nearer the slack (fig.6).

If your warp is really slack you should cut off the excess which has been worked around, and re-tie it as near as possible to the nail at the top of the frame.

Warping up the frame. Use two threads together, taking them once around each nail. Keep an even tension.

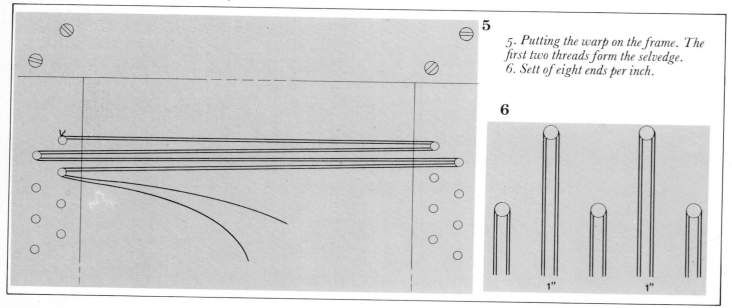

5

5. Putting the warp on the frame. The first two threads form the selvedge.
6. Sett of eight ends per inch.

6

1"   1"

Inserting cross sticks

After adjusting the warp tension the two cross sticks are inserted. The sticks maintain the order of the threads right across the warp and make it easier to weave. They also make a useful barrier against which to weave. The two sticks are inserted near the nails at the bottom of the frame.

Take the first stick and place the first two threads of the selvedge on top of it. It does not matter which side you start from.

The next warp goes under the stick, the next over and so on across the warp. The odd warp ends are now all on top of the stick and the evens underneath (fig.8).

The second stick is inserted with the odds and evens reversed and the threads form a cross between the two sticks when viewed from the side. Care should be taken to prevent the threads from getting out of sequence when the sticks are put in.

This procedure is really very simple, though at first glance it may seem complicated. You must, however, take special care to insure that all your initial preparations in setting up the loom and warping it ready for use are accurate.

All the weaving you do, whether you follow our design for the sampler or create a design of your own, will depend for its finished result on these initial stages, so it is well worth taking a little trouble and time before you start. Once the cross sticks have been inserted you are ready to begin weaving the design for the sampler.

Although this loom is specially designed to fit the sampler we give, there is no reason why you can't use it to weave designs of your own or to make up small items. It is important for really creative tapestry not to build in your own restrictions and conventions. From our instructions you can make up your own cartoons and use the basic principles to draw up almost any design.

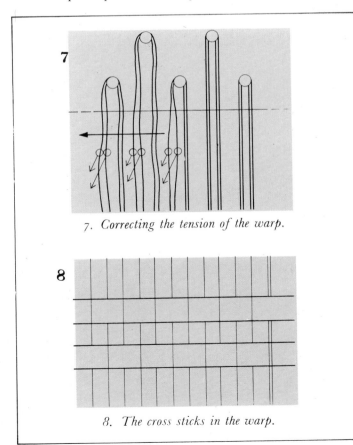

7. Correcting the tension of the warp.

8. The cross sticks in the warp.

If you follow the instructions in this chapter you can build a versatile frame loom for tapestry weaving, but you can still achieve interesting effects on a very small frame. Use a wool yarn for the warp, and begin and end the weaving with a few rows of yarn. In between, any strips can be used—from metallic cord to velvet. Either weave single strips or use a continuous length. Machine stitch all around the weaving after cutting the warp ends, so that the piece remains secure.

Weaving a sampler

There are various tapestry techniques which are used to create the definition between color and image. The sampler shown incorporates the basic shapes—lines, diagonals, circles, diamonds—which you will need when you are creating your own designs. Even the most elaborate medieval pictorial tapestries used these basic methods to create their intricate images.

For clarity only two colors are used, but you will find that a different range of colors can transform a design into something different.

Making a cartoon

Before starting to weave a tapestry it is often advisable to work out the design on paper. Many weavers find it helpful to make the paper design the same size as the final tapestry and to hang it behind the warp threads of the loom as a pattern from which to weave. This kind of accurate full-scale pattern is known as a cartoon.

To make the cartoon
You will need
☐ A sheet of white paper 29 inches by 16 inches.
☐ Black felt-tipped pen or black gummed paper.
Mark the paper off into 1 inch squares.
Each of the squares on your paper is represented by a square in fig.1.

Using the felt pen or the gummed paper, black in the relevant squares.

Pin this behind your frame loom so that you have an outline to follow.

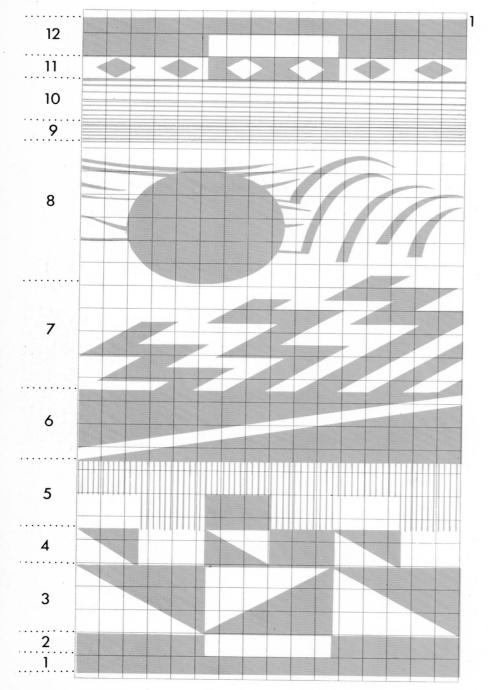

Above: The finished tapestry.
Right: The designer of the sampler, David Hill, working at his loom with the cartoon positioned behind the warp threads.

1. The pattern for the tapestry sampler. Each small square represents 1 inch square, when making a full size cartoon to hang behind the loom.

2

2. Tapestry bobbin wound with yarn.

Working from the bottom to the top, you must mark the sampler into sections.

The Tapestry sampler
An elegant wall hanging, 28½ inches by 16 inches, which combines most basic tapestry shapes.

For the sampler
You will need
☐ ¼lb of black and white rug wool (3-ply).
  If three-ply rug wool is unavailable ask your supplier for an alternative. A two-ply wool, for instance, with a different twist, may be suitable.
☐ Frame loom, 3 feet 6 inches by 2 feet, warped with warp cotton or heavy crochet cotton, 8 ends per in.
☐ About six 4 inch tapestry bobbins.
  Tapestry bobbins can be difficult to obtain and many weavers do not use them. The sampler can be worked without any bobbins at all, but the pointed end of the bobbin is useful for beating down the weft between the warp. It is worth finding out if you like to work with one.

Preparing the weft
Wind some of the black weft yarn tightly around a tapestry bobbin (fig.2). Be careful not to overfill the bobbin—apart from the difficulty in passing it through the warp, there is also the danger of yarn slipping off.

Alternatively, the yarn may be wound into a tight cylindrical shape instead of onto a bobbin (fig.3).

Section One
The first section of the tapestry is a solid ¾ inch band of black. This section not only gives you a chance to practice weaving, but the rows of plain weaving also serve to space the warp threads evenly.

Weaving from right to left
To start off your weaving, hold the bobbin in the right hand and use the left hand to 'make a shed' (to lift alternate warp ends so that the bobbin can be passed behind them).

To make the shed
Start about 2 inches in from the right selvedge picking up the alternate threads with the thumb and first finger of the left hand. The two threads at the end should be treated as one as they form the selvedge.

Then by thrusting the left hand into the horizontal position behind these threads, a space (the shed) can be made between those warp ends in front of the hand and those behind.

Pass the bobbin through the space created and from the right hand to the left.

Keep the bobbin vertical to prevent too much weft from unwinding.

Continue this process by weaving small sections until the left hand side is reached. The last two threads should also be treated as one to form the other selvedge.

Tension: When the weft has been passed through do not pull it tight, but form a small loop (fig.4a). It is important to leave this loop before beating down, as tightly pulled weft will result in the edges of the tapestry moving inwards as well as making it difficult to cover the warp properly. On the other hand, if you leave too big a loop the width of the warp will begin to increase and

loops will stick out from the face of the weaving. The correct amount of slack will be achieved with practice.

After forming the loop, beat it down with the point of the bobbin (while holding the bobbin end of the weft), as shown (figs.4b and 4c).

Weaving from left to right
Pass the weft around two threads of the left hand selvedge.

With the fingers of the right hand, lift the warp ends which lay behind the weft in the previous pick (row).

Make the shed by thrusting the hand into the horizontal position as before, and pass the bobbin through from the left to the right hand.

Selvedges
During the weaving, care must be taken to keep the selvedges firm and straight.

Then after each ½ inch of weaving, take the weft twice around each selvedge (fig.5).

This is necessary because the weft usually beats down more closely at the selvedge and this adjusts the level.

If any difficulty is experienced in preventing the edge of the tapestry from moving inwards, they can be kept straight by lacing the selvedges to the side of the weaving frame (fig.6).

Joining threads
When the weft yarn which is wound around the bobbin comes to an end, the last 2 inches are left hanging down either at the front or at the back of the tapestry. The beginning of the next length of weft is started next to the end of the last length, again leaving 2 inches hanging on the same side.

Traditionally, tapestries were woven back to front with all the ends hanging down the side facing the weaver. However, these ends tend to obscure what is happening and you may find it easier to work with the front facing you. There is no need to overlap the beginnings and ends of the weft, as tapestry weave is very firm and the ends will not pull out.

Beating
After weaving the ¾ inch of black, the weft must be beaten down more closely. Use a heavy tapestry fork to do this (fig.7).

Tapestry Weave
The aim of the conventional tapestry weave is to cover

Pick up alternate warp ends and thrust your hand into the shed to hold the two sets of threads apart.

3

3. If you do not have a bobbin, the yarn can be wound into a cylindrical shape.

4a, b, c. Leave a loop of weft and beat with the point of the bobbin.

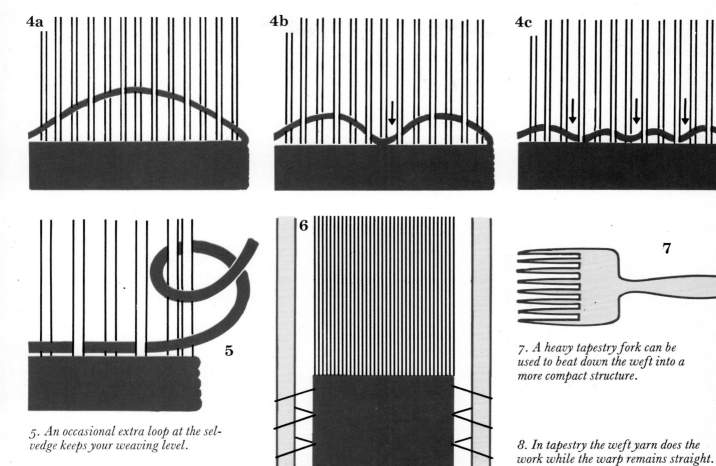

4a

4b

4c

5

6

7

7. A heavy tapestry fork can be used to beat down the weft into a more compact structure.

5. An occasional extra loop at the selvedge keeps your weaving level.

6. To stop your tapestry going in you can lace it to the side of the frame.

8. In tapestry the weft yarn does the work while the warp remains straight.

8

warp

weft

Pass the bobbin or yarn bundle from one hand to the other through the shed. Pull the wool gently through.

Leave a small loop of thread so that the weft is not too taut. Beat down the slack with the point of the bobbin.

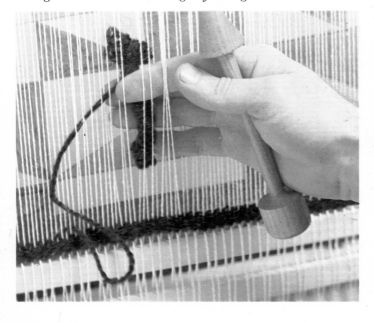

the warp fully and compactly with the weft. Unlike most other weaves where the warp and weft bend around each other, tapestry keeps the vertical warp threads straight, with the weft bending around them to form the fabric (fig.8). The warp is completely covered and the weft alone creates the design.

Section Two

The width of the warp is now divided into three equal parts in the design. The black weft is continued up to the two outside thirds for 1 inch and a white weft is introduced into the middle third.

To create a clear-cut division between the three areas of color you will have to join the black and white wefts in the vertical line.

Joining vertically

There are three basic methods of joining two sections of weft to make a vertical line.

Method 1

The simplest way of making a vertical join is to pass the colored wefts around a single warp end (fig.1). This method soon leads to a build-up of weft around the common warp and consequent bulge in the weaving.

Method 2

Paradoxically, this build-up can be decreased if alternate groups of three weft picks (rows) are looped around the same warp end (fig.2). The subsequent beating down will dovetail the loops into each other in the form of a point (fig.3). However, the saw-toothed effect is increased.

Method 3

A modification of this join, which is the one used in section two, joins the black and white wefts over three warps (fig.4). This method of joining is strong and because the join is staggered over three warp ends it can be continued for any height without fear of build-up.

To make the vertical join

Starting with the left side black weft, weave up to the warp end 2 (fig.5). This is the middle end of the three around which the join will be formed.

Pass the weft around it and return to the left selvedge.

Return with the black weft and go around warp end 1. Return it to the selvedge.

As you can see from fig.5, it is necessary to weave both the black and white pieces alternately to make the join, and a strict order of weaving must be maintained. This process is more complicated than it seems at first glance because Section Two has two joins and both must be worked together, as the white center weft plays its part in each join.

The whole width of the warp must be worked step by step as both joins must be formed at the same time.

Taking the white weft, which should start from the right hand side of the center third, weave until end 3 is reached (fig.5).

Take the white weft around end 3 and return to the other side of the white section.

As the join has also to be repeated on the right hand side, pass the white weft around warp end 5 as shown (fig.5).

Return the white weft to the left hand side and pass it around end 2.

Start the black weft on the right hand side and weave up to and around end 6.

Continue this process for 1 inch, making the two joins simultaneously. Do not forget to beat down well with the point of your bobbin.

1. A simple join around one warp end.
2–3. Three threads around one warp.
4–5. Making a join around three warps.

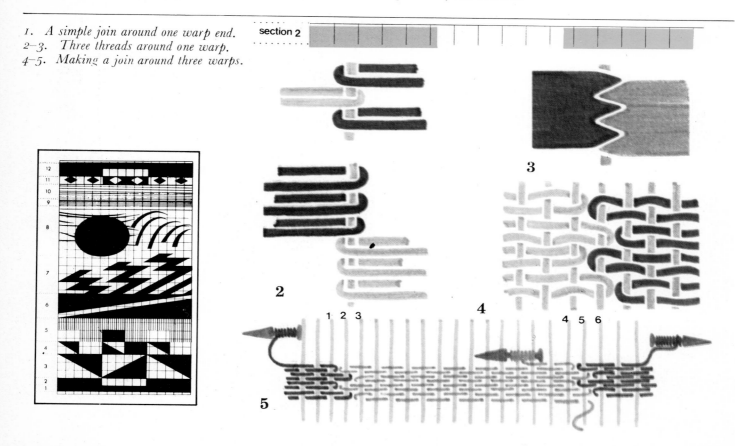

section 3

6. *A steep incline is produced when more than one weft is passed around each warp end.*
7. *A gradual incline is produced by reducing the number of warp ends covered by each weft pick.*

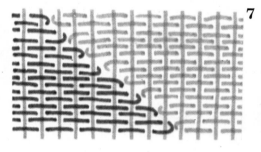

7

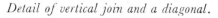

Detail of vertical join and a diagonal.

Section Three

In this section, the vertical joins between the three main sections are made as in Section Two, method 3. The triangles are woven by increasing or decreasing the number of warp ends covered by each pick.

Diagonals

The angle of incline of the diagonal is controlled either by the number of times the weft is taken around the same warp end (fig.6) or by reducing the number of warp ends covered by the weft by one or more at a time (fig.7). The first method produces a steep incline, the second a flatter one. In Section Three, the increase and decrease is by one warp end (fig.7).

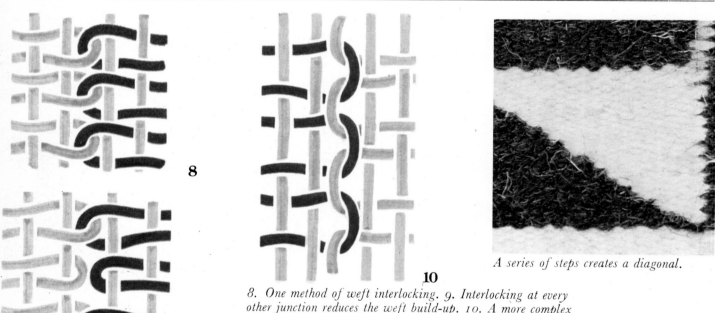

8

9

10

8. *One method of weft interlocking.* 9. *Interlocking at every other junction reduces the weft build-up.* 10. *A more complex method of weft interlocking.*

A series of steps creates a diagonal.

section 4

Section Four

The diagonals are woven as in the previous section, increasing and decreasing by one warp end. The method used here for weaving the vertical join is by weft interlocking. This method gives the best definition between the two colors.

Weft interlocking
Method 1

The first method is formed by interlocking the black and white weft picks between the two warp ends (fig.8). The two colors always interlock in the same direction to insure the clearest division between the two colors. A certain amount of build-up will occur with this method.

Method 2

A variation on this is the method used in the sampler. The interlocking occurs at every other junction of the two colors (fig.9). This prevents any build-up and has the added advantage of being quick to weave.

Method 3

The third system of interlocking also gives a clearly-defined division between the two colors (fig.10). This is slightly more complex and time consuming, but the resultant join is very solid and firm.

Rows in alternate colors form stripes.

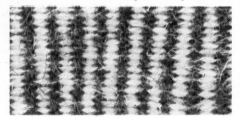

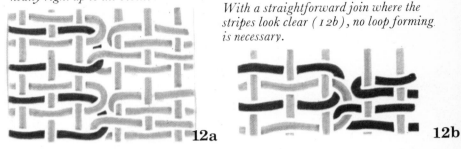

section 5

12. You may find that joins between stripes and blocks sometimes look muddled and ill-defined (as in 12a). To make the join between them sharper, leave enough slack on the black yarn so that you can build up the white picks (P) and draw the black yarn into a loop at the back. This makes the stripes run neatly right up to the block.

11. Forming vertical stripes.

With a straightforward join where the stripes look clear (12b), no loop forming is necessary.

11

12a

12b

Section Five

The vertical joins between the three blocks of solid color and the black and white stripes are made in the same way as the verticals in method two of Section Four.

Vertical Stripes

Weaving vertical stripes is very simple.

Weave one pick with the black weft and then one pick with the white. After a few rows you will notice that the

black and white wefts respectively always cover the same warp ends, thus producing the striped effect (fig.11).

In the first part of the section, where the stripes are between the solid colors, a little practice will be needed in order to weave neat divisions at the vertical joins (fig.12).

When the top of the solid color blocks is reached, continue the striped effect across the whole width of the warp.

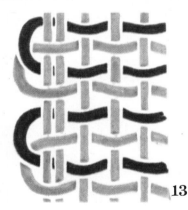

13

Your tapestry should have a neat straight edge. If not check your tension.
13. Locking at the selvedges.
14. An advanced technique for selvedges.

14

Selvedges

When weaving one pick of one color followed by a pick of another color, cross one over the other at the selvedge so that they lock (fig.13), or else the selvedge will be missed.

A neater way of forming the selvedge is to leave a loop

which is pulled around the selvedge to the back of the tapestry by the other weft color (fig.14). With this method, the crossing of the wefts is not shown and the striped effect is continued right to the edge.

The diagonal stripe is actually a series of small steps.

section 6

1. Creating a gradual incline.

1

Section Six

This section of diagonals is woven using the technique shown in Section Three. However, here the rate of increase is by four warp ends per pick (fig.1). This creates a gradual slope.

Do not forget that the white diagonal stripe is increased on one side while being decreased on the other.

Take special care here, to maintain tension.

Each square is 1 inch square in the graph sections.

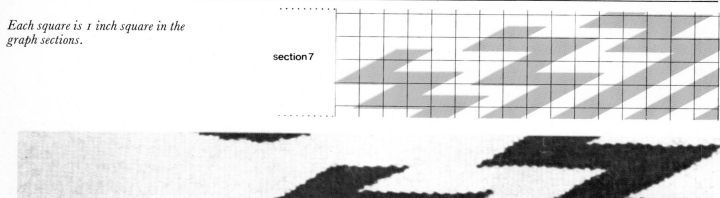

section 7

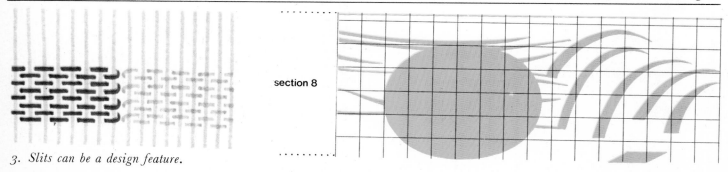

Section Seven

This area has been included for practice in weaving the shapes already mentioned. The forms are more complex, and several bobbins of weft must be worked together. In tapestry small areas can be worked independently. It is not always necessary to build up the whole of the warp at any one time. However, you must always have woven the area directly underneath the area you are working.

section 8

3. Slits can be a design feature.

2

3. *Graduating steps form curved lines.*

Watch your cartoon for the position of the lines coming out from the circle.

3

Section Eight
This section is complicated as it combines several different shapes.

Before you start to weave this area, read all the instructions. For clarity, the instructions for the circle have been dealt with in isolation. When you actually come to weave, you will have to combine the circle with the small black lines radiating from it.

Weaving a circle
Before beginning to weave a circular shape it is advisable to mark out the shape on the warp with a broad felt-tipped pen. The curve of the circle is woven using a combination of diagonal and vertical weft joining.

Start by weaving the white background. Two separate bobbins of white will be required, one for working the left side and the other for the right.

From the centre of the bottom curve, start weaving the background on one side, gradually increasing the slope by the method explained for weaving diagonals (fig. 2).

There will not be a regular increase as there is with triangles and you will have to follow the outline of the circle on the warp. Remember to weave slightly higher than the outline to make up for the loss when beating down.

Continue the increasing until the weft is passing three times around a single warp end.

Weave the background on the other side in the same manner. The lower portion of the black circle can now be woven up to the level of the background.

From this point in weaving the circle, vertical weft joining should be used for weaving the steepest part of the circle. You can choose any of the methods described. Both background wefts and circle weft should be built up together.

As the steepness of the slope declines (from the point where the black weft is passing three times around a single warp end), continue weaving the circle by modifying the steepness of the diagonal weave until the circle is complete.

Remember, these instructions are for weaving a circle with a plain background. As the sampler has black stripes coming out of it, these will have to be woven in as you weave the circle.

Horizontal thin stripes
These come out from the circle and are woven by continuing the black weft from the circle into the background for two, and occasionally three picks.

Watching out for the stripes, weave the circle and the background, following the instructions given for weaving the circle.

The black curved lines
These on the right-hand side are formed by using the circle techniques. The steep part is woven with the weft going four times around one warp end without any interlocking. This type of join forms small slits (fig. 3).

In all cases where verticals are used they can be woven in this manner with the resulting slits becoming a design feature, as in Kelim rugs. Alternatively, they can be sewn up afterwards at the back.

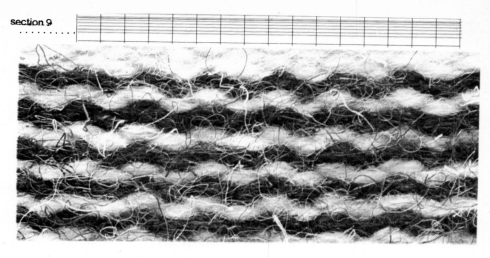

*Detail of the horizontal stripes formed
by weaving two picks of each color.*

4. How to keep a neat selvedge.

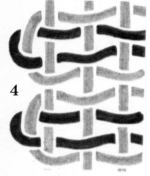

4

Section Nine

The thin slightly wavy lines are created by weaving two picks of black, followed by two picks of white and so on.

To avoid unsightly loops at the selvedges cover the weft not being used by the working weft (fig.4).

A neat selvedge makes all the difference to the work.

*The shading effect is created by increasing
the number of white picks.*

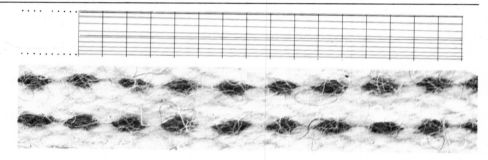

Section Ten

Weave three picks of white, one pick of black, followed by three of white, one of black and so on.

Continue this for about ½ inch.

Increase the number of white weft picks to five but still only weave one pick of black.

Extend the blocks of white to seven and then nine picks, at regular intervals, to give a progressive shading effect from dark to light.

Once again carry the black weft up the selvedge, covering it with the white as in the previous section (fig.4), until the black is required again.

*Weave each diamond with its back-
ground so that you can beat down.*

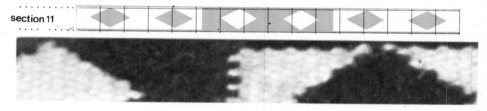

Section Eleven

At this point, the width of the warp is again divided into three equal parts. The diamond shapes, black on white, white on black, are woven using the normal diagonal technique, and the vertical joins by method 3, Section Two.

*In the final stage the tightening warp
threads will need more care in covering.*

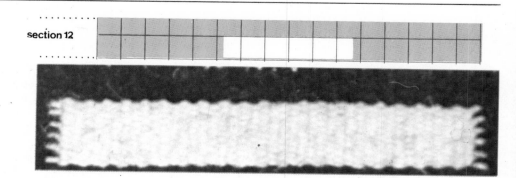

Section Twelve

The last part of the sampler is a repeat of the first two sections. This is a 1 inch area divided into three blocks, two black on the outsides and white in the center. This is followed by ¾ inch of plain black.

Taking tapestry off the loom

Cut the warp from the frame leaving a sufficient length of warp, about 3 inches, to allow for tying knots. At the bottom of the tapestry this normally means cutting the warp as near to the nails as possible.

There are several ways in which the edge can be finished off. If the edge is to be turned under and sewn, then the ends of the warp can be cut much closer.

The simplest method is to tie a series of overhand knots (fig.5). Make sure you get the knot as close to the weaving as possible.

Because tapestry is such a firm compact weave, it is not absolutely necessary to darn in the loose weft ends. If you leave them loose, trim them down to a tidy length of about 2 inches.

Brush lightly to get rid of any loose fibers which may be still clinging to the surface of the tapestry. As it is pure wool and cotton, you can wash your tapestry gently when it gets dirty

5

5. Finishing off the tapestry with a series of overhand knots.
Leave the fringe long if you wish it to be a design feature.

Overleaf: A 17th century English silk embroidery on canvas, showing the Old Testament story of Esther. By permission of the Victoria and Albert Museum.

The final tapestry should have straight even edges. If they are pulled in, careful stretching with an iron may help.

23

Introduction to needlepoint

From the time that someone called the famous Bayeux panel a tapestry, people have been confused about what is embroidery, what is tapestry and what is needlepoint. In fact, the Bayeux panel is an example of early English embroidery, worked in wools on a linen fabric. Tapestry is always woven, in patterns and pictures, on a loom, with small sections woven individually, then stitched together by hand. When next you visit a museum, look carefully at the tapestries and you'll see how small some sections are. Needlepoint is embroidery on canvas. It was very popular in England and Europe from the early sixteenth century until the mid-eighteenth century, but then it marked time, until it was recently revived.

Now the lovely variety of traditional needlepoint stitches, which have for so long been neglected, are enjoying a new importance. They are being used in fabulous modern designs, often with unusual new yarns which were not formerly associated with embroidery.

Today, needlepoint is an adventure in the use of stitches, yarns, and abstract designs which lend themselves to the square formation of the stitches.

Colorful, textured and tough

The attraction of needlepoint today, apart from the fact that it is hand-made and not mass produced, is that all-over embroidery on canvas makes objects and decorations which are really tough and hard-wearing.

It is simple to do, and you have only to visit the yarn counter of any shop to be inspired. Brilliant silks, metallic threads, stranded shiny cottons, soft matt cottons, new nubbly-textured wools and modern synthetics all come in a myriad of beautiful colors.

As well as the color, the success of all needlepoint depends upon the texture of the stitches and the threads.

Canvas size

The canvas must be firm, supple, and evenly woven, and the number of threads to an inch can vary from 24 per inch for fine work, to $3\frac{1}{2}$ per inch for very coarse work. There are two types, single thread canvas called Mono-canvas and double thread canvas called Penelope. You can also use evenly woven fabrics such as Aida cloth, or Hardanger, and even-weave linens or woolen fabrics. Single thread canvas is measured by the number of threads to the inch and double thread canvas is measured to the number of double threads to the inch. Single weave canvas is the best to use since it is possible to embroider a wide variety of stitches on it, whereas double weave is restricted to 4 or 5 only.

Needles

Use tapestry needles with large eyes and blunt points. They are available in a variety of sizes, of which sizes 18-22 are the most popular, but size 14 is better for very coarse material.

Floral design, typical of nineteenth century needlepoint, with soft muted colors, careful shading, and an ornate over-all appearance. Threads of canvas have been separated to produce petit point for fine, delicate stitches

Frames

Needlepoint should be worked in a frame. This helps you to maintain the correct shape of the work while it is being embroidered. Small items which you can easily hold in your hand need not be framed.

Yarns

In needlepoint the stitches must completely cover the canvas. Yarns are available in differing thicknesses and some are made up of several individual strands which are twisted together but can be separated as required. To cover the canvas you need to use the correct thickness of yarn. If, however, the thread coverage looks thin and mean, you should pad it out with the technique known as tramming to fill the space. Never use too long a yarn as it will wear thin and your work will look uneven and tired. If you find the yarn becoming thin or fluffy, start a new length of yarn at once. It is usually quicker to use a short length—which is a yarn about 12 to 14 inches long.

A modern cushion, designed by Joan Nicholson, with abstract pattern repeats, and clear bright colors which blend well together

The right yarn for the canvas

1. Double thread canvas
12 double threads to 1 inch shown.
Yarns: tapestry wool, crewel wool, 4-ply knitting yarns, Pearl cotton, 6 strand floss, metallic yarns, stranded pure silk.

2. Double thread canvas
10 double threads to 1 inch shown.
Yarns as for No 1 plus knitting worsted, modern synthetics.

3. Petit point canvas
20 threads to 1 inch shown.
Yarns as for No 1.

4. Single weave canvas
18 threads to 1 inch shown.
Yarns as for No 1 and No 2 plus knitting yarns in a variety of textures such as mohair, tweed, metallic and wool mixtures, soft embroidery cotton, rug wool, applied braids and cords, weaving yarns.

5. Single weave
12 threads to 1 inch.
Yarns as for No 1 and No 2 and No 4 using more than one thickness of yarn where necessary plus fine ribbons, strings.

Check off your canvas information against the picture on the right

The right stitch for the right texture

Any design loses impact if all the areas are worked in the same texture, that is, all rough or all smooth. For the most pleasing effect, it is important to separate areas of the design into smooth, medium and rough textures. (Tent, Gobelin, straight and satin stitches are all smooth. Cross-stitch, rice and star stitches are all semi-rough. Double cross, oblong and tufted stitches are very rough.) Some stitches lend themselves to particular textures and shapes. For instance, diagonal bricking and Smyrna cross stitch have a good texture for walls and brickwork, herringbone fillings interpret water very well and Surry stitch is a good stitch for the curves of flowers or for furry textures. Tent and Gobelin stitches clarify the line of a design and for any form of intricate, realistic shading, nothing beats tent stitch.

Strong texture often looks most effective when it is used sparingly. For example, you could work just the mane and tail of a horse in a rough textured stitch, or use different stitches for flower centers and leaves, or the underside of a fish.

How to start

1. Find the center of the piece of canvas by folding it in half, horizontally and vertically; mark the center lightly with a colored crayon or thread. Start in the center, but instead of using a knot, draw the needle up through the canvas, leaving a tail about half an inch long at the back.
2. Hold this thread closely to the canvas and work over it, binding it in with the first few stitches (which are seen here from the back).

To finish off

Darn the thread into the stitches at the back of your work to secure it. To continue with a new thread, darn its tail into the back of the previous row.

Never allow any of these threads to accumulate in one place as this results in unsightly bumps.

Instructions for making up needlepoint

Sometimes needlepoint, which takes quite a time to complete, can be ruined by hurried making up, so in order to avoid spoiling your careful work follow these instructions.

Blocking

It is essential to allow for blocking purposes at least 2 inches of canvas all around the finished size of the work. The excess canvas is trimmed away to the required seam width after blocking. Needlepoint should never be pressed with an iron, as this flattens the textured stitches and ruins the appearance. Most stitches distort the canvas because of their diagonal pull and the best way to restore the canvas to its original shape is as follows: Dampen the back of the work with cold water. Cover a drawing board, or old work table with several sheets of white blotting paper. Place the work face down on the board and pin out, using rust-proof thumb tacks at 1 inch intervals. Pull the work gently into shape, adjusting the thumb tacks. Dampen the work again thoroughly and leave for at least 24 hours, away from heat, until it is dry. When the work is completely dry, check for any missed stitches and fill them in at this stage.

This sampler is worked in tent stitch, slanted Gobelin, bricking, Parisian, Hungarian, upright Gobelin

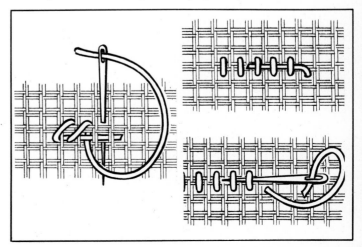

How to make a seam

There are several seam methods suitable for needlepoint and this one is particularly good for small items which cannot be turned through to the right side after being seamed. The usual seam allowance is $\frac{5}{8}$ inch, but for smaller items, such as lighter cases, $\frac{3}{8}$ inch is sufficient. As needlepoint frays easily it is a good idea to overcast the raw edges before making up. With imaginative use of yarn and stitches, the seams can form a complementary and decorative feature to the piece of work.

Method

Trim the canvas ready to seam and fold all turnings to the wrong side of the work. Trim and neaten the corners and baste the seam allowance in place. Pin the two seam edges with the wrong sides together, matching up the pattern. Work whip stitch, cross-stitch or oblong cross-stitch along the seam on the right side, picking up opposite threads of the canvas from each side as you work. The seam when completed becomes part of the needlepoint.

Linings

The choice of a lining is most important since it should not draw attention away from the stitching, either in color or texture. It is best to choose a firm dull surface fabric in a plain toning color. Pick the darkest tone used in the design because this will give strength to the design, whereas a light color will draw more attention to the lining than to the needlepoint. Lining seams can either be machine stitched or hand sewn with back-stitch.

Using a chart

A chart demands a little concentration when it comes to plotting the outlines, but once these are worked out the rest is easy. Start by finding the center of the chart.
Count the number of squares from top to bottom and side to side, divide each total by half and mark the center with a pencil or lines of basting. Start counting and stitching from the center. Each square on the chart corresponds to one thread intersection on the canvas.
If there are large areas of color to be filled in, mark an outline and the smaller areas first, and then fill in the larger areas.

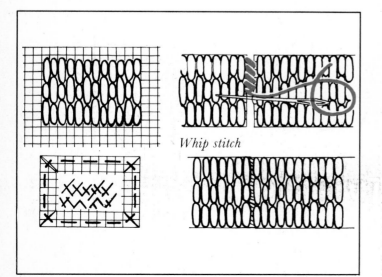

Whip stitch

Basic stitch library

Cross-stitches

Cross-stitch comes in so many guises that part of the fun of working it is to find how many adaptations you can invent. When working a sampler include as many different stitches as you can so that your work is interesting to look at. Or, use one variation of cross-stitch to bring a plain tent stitch picture to life.
The illustrations on these pages have been enlarged beyond life size so that each stitch is clear. When they are seen in scale the stitches will cover the canvas completely.

Cross-stitch

To work cross-stitch make a row of slanting stitches from left to right and then make another row from right to left on top of them. The picture shows the stitch worked with a thin wool so that you can clearly see how it builds up but of course, worked correctly, the canvas should be completely covered with yarn. Each cross-stitch should add up to a perfect square and must always be worked over an equal number of threads, down and across. The main point to remember is that the upper stitches must always lie in the same direction.

Method of working cross-stitch

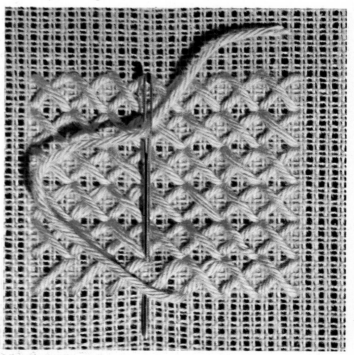

Half cross-stitch

Half cross-stitch is hard-wearing—smooth, flat and ideal for things which need to be tough, like stool and chair seats. But because it is simple to do, it is one of the best stitches to use for any small scale patterns. This stitch is worked as shown, from left to right. Up through the canvas from bottom left, down through the next hole on top right. This makes a diagonal stitch on the front and a short straight stitch on the back.

Fasten off at the end of each area of color and begin again so that you do not leave long lengths of yarn at the back.

Half cross-stitch. The drawing shows the method used when working in a frame. The right hand is always on the top of the work, the left hand at the bottom

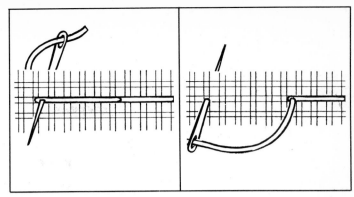

The stitch worked over tramming

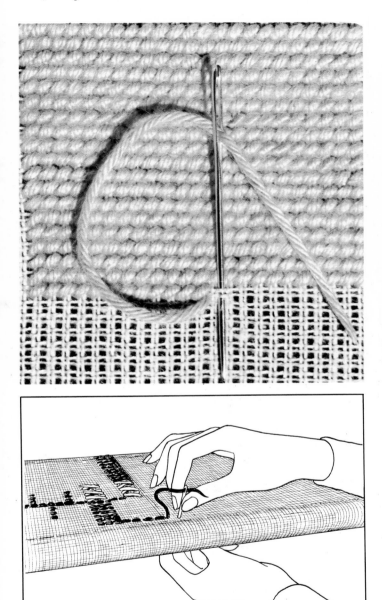

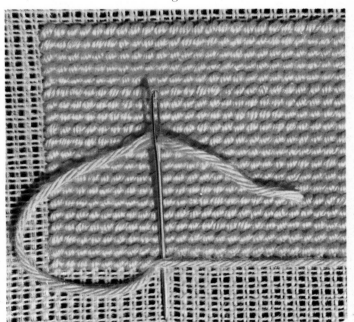

Tent stitch or petit point

Bring the needle through to the right side and then take it back down one thread further on. Continue to the end of the row and then work backward and forward until the area is filled. If the work is spread over a large area it is advisable to work the stitch diagonally to prevent the canvas from being pulled out of shape. Take the needle back over 1 thread and forward 2 threads, making a longer thread on the back of the work than on the front. The stitch can also be worked in vertical or horizontal lines in alternate directions, that is, with the stitches sloping from left to right in one row and right to left in the next. When this method is used, it is called reverse tent stitch.

Tent stitch—horizontal, diagonal and reversed

Tramming

Tramming is a padding stitch which is used when the yarn is not thick enough to cover the canvas completely.

The tramming yarn runs along each horizontal single canvas thread or pairs of threads (called "tramlines") as shown in the illustration. Bring the yarn up through these tramlines, leaving the short tail at the back. Work in overlapping tramming stitches, not more than 4 inches long for the length of your working area. Then take the yarn down again through the tramlines. Work the stitch over the tramming yarn, binding in the tramming tails as you go.

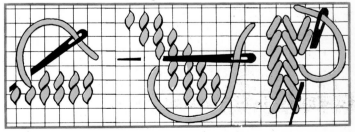

NB Petit-point is a smaller version of Tent stitch. The patterns in the following pages describe these as two separate stitches to make it easier to follow the charts.

Oblong cross-stitch

Work in the same way as ordinary cross-stitch but bring the needle through the 5th hole down from the top of the work. Insert the needle 4 holes up, 2 across. Bring the needle through 4 holes down.

Oblong cross-stitch covers the canvas quickly and has an elegant look

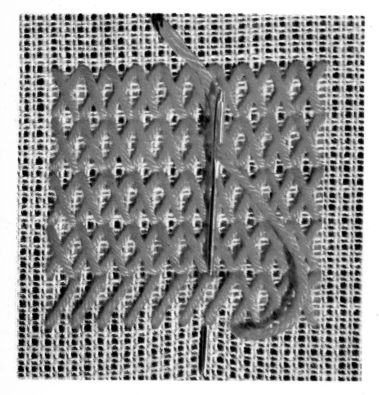

Oblong cross-stitch with bars

Begin by working oblong cross-stitch then work bars one row from right to left, the next row from left to right and so on. Bring the needle through the 3rd hole down, 3rd in from the edge of work. Insert needle 2 holes back. Bring needle through 4 holes on. Repeat to end of row.

Oblong cross-stitch with bars for a chunkier look

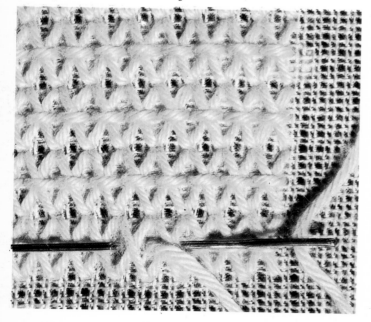

Long-legged cross-stitch

This differs from ordinary cross-stitch only in that one of the crossing stitches is worked over twice as many threads as the other. Bring the needle through the 4th hole down from the top of the work. *Insert needle 8 holes across, 4 holes up. Bring needle through 4 holes down. Insert needle 4 holes up, 4 back. Bring needle through 4 holes down. Repeat from * to end of row.

Long-legged cross-stitch, a simple but effective variation

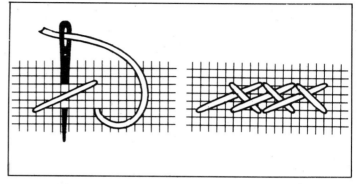

Double cross-stitch

In this stitch each star is completed before starting the next. To work one star bring the needle through at the top left-hand side of work. Insert needle 4 holes down, 4 across. Bring needle through 4 holes up. Insert needle 4 holes down, 4 back. Bring needle through 4 holes up, 2 across. Insert needle 4 holes down. Bring needle through 2 holes up, 2 back. Insert needle 4 holes across.

Double cross-stitch turns each stitch into an eight-pointed star

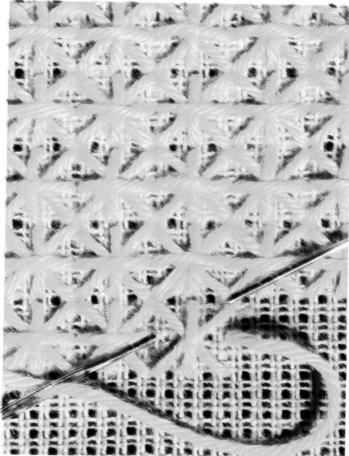

Alternating cross-stitch

This filling stitch is composed of two cross-stitches of different sizes in interlocking rows.

Work from right to left. Bring needle through 3rd hole down from top of work. Insert needle 1 hole up, 1 across. Bring needle through 2 holes down. Insert needle 3 holes up, 1 across. Bring needle through 2 holes down. Repeat to end of row. To complete the crosses work the return row from left to right. Next row—bring needle through 4 holes down and work each row so that it interlocks with the one above by working the top of each stitch into the same holes as the bottom of the stitch above.

Alternating cross-stitch, a filling with lots of texture interest

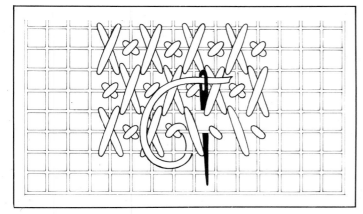

Rice stitch

This is a filling stitch which can be worked in one or two colors (here it is shown worked in two). It consists of ordinary cross-stitch with the arms crossed by bars of half cross-stitch in the same or a different color.

Work the area in ordinary cross-stitch then work the first row of bars from left to right. Bring needle through 3rd hole down from top of work. Insert needle 2 holes down, 2 across, to the right. Bring needle through 2 holes up, 2 across. Insert needle 2 holes down, 2 across to the right. Repeat to the end of the row. Then repeat the process entirely from right to left to complete the row.

Rice stitch can be worked in one color only or two contrasting shades

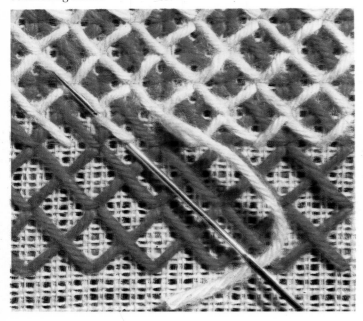

Italian cross-stitch

Work in rows from left to right, starting at the bottom left of the shape which is to be filled.

Work each stitch in 4 movements as shown in the diagram—bring needle through in the bottom left-hand corner of the work. Insert needle 3 holes across. Bring needle through 1st hole again. Insert needle 3 holes up, 3 across and bring it through the 1st hole again. Insert needle 3 holes up. Bring needle through 3 holes down, 3 across. Insert needle 3 holes up, 3 back. Bring needle up 3 holes down, 3 across. Continue these movements to the end of the row, making a final upright stitch. Work another row above, also from left to right. This will complete the previous row.

Italian cross-stitch sets each cross in its own square frame

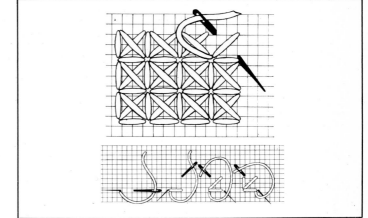

Chain stitch method 1

This is a very quick method worked with a fine crochet hook, skipping 2 holes of the canvas with every stitch. For a shorter stitch skip 1 hole each time; for a longer one, skip more. Do not make the stitches too long or the work will wear badly. When one row is completed, finish off and start again with the next unless continuing in the same color, in which case turn the work and commence the next row. It is essential to finish ends securely because if they work loose a whole row of stitching will come undone.

Work chain stitch 2 like chain stitch in embroidery as shown in the illustration. Finish the end of each row with a small stitch to hold the last chain in place. Once again, finish off the thread securely.

Chain stitch method 1   *Chain stitch method 2*

31

Plaited Gobelin stitch

This stitch is worked in horizontal rows over 4 threads up and 2 across to the left. Work to the length of the area you want to cover, leaving a space of 2 threads between each stitch. The second row is worked 2 threads down and in the opposite direction, giving a plaited or woven effect.

Plaited Gobelin Stitch

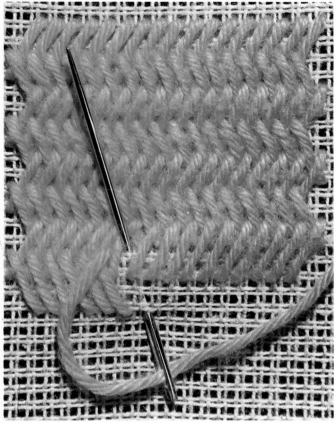

Stem stitch

Work from the bottom upward over 2 horizontal threads and 2 vertical threads. The spaces between the rows are filled with backstitches in a yarn of contrasting colors.

Stem stitch

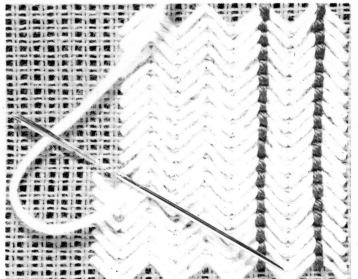

Mosaic stitch

This is worked in diagonal rows from top left to bottom right of the canvas in groups of 3 stitches; over 1, 2 and 1 threads of canvas.

Mosaic stitch

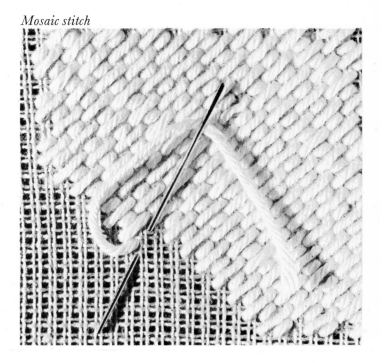

Mosaic diamond stitch

This is worked in rows from left to right over 1, 3, 5, 3, and 1 threads of canvas.

Mosaic diamond stitch

Upright Gobelin

This is worked with straight up-and-down stitches, usually over 4 horizontal threads of canvas.

Slanted Gobelin

This is similar to upright Gobelin, but worked over 2 vertical and 4 horizontal threads.

Bricking

This upright stitch is worked in interlocking rows.

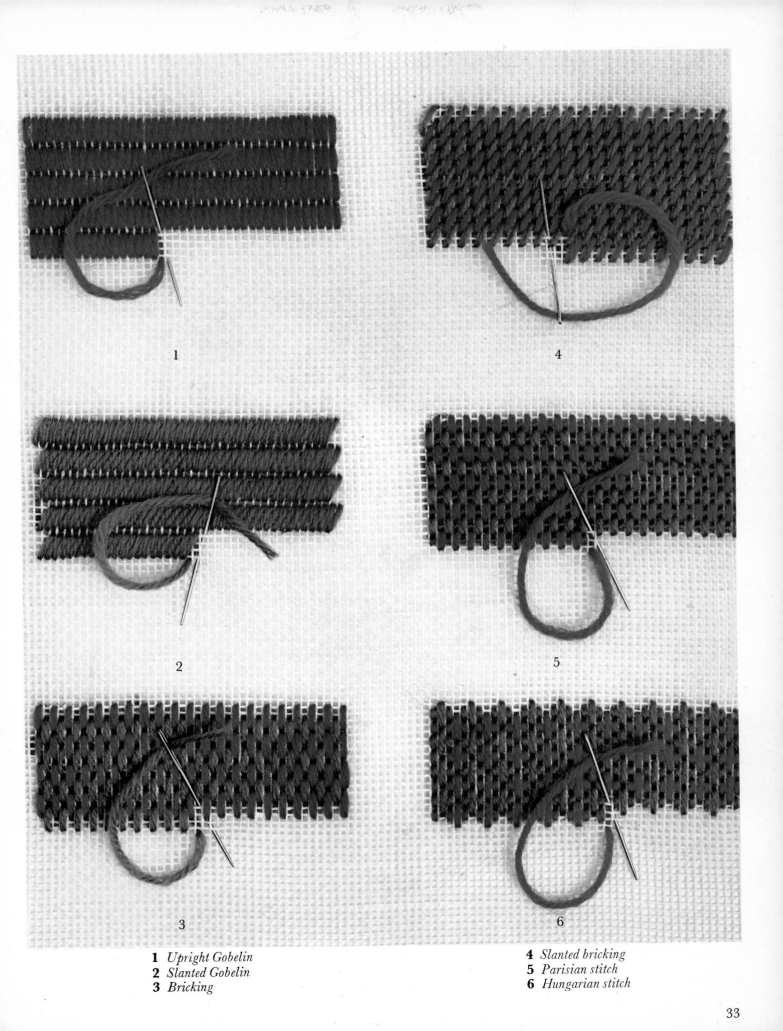

1 Upright Gobelin
2 Slanted Gobelin
3 Bricking

4 Slanted bricking
5 Parisian stitch
6 Hungarian stitch

1st row. Work stitches over 4 horizontal threads leaving a space between each stitch.

2nd row. Start 2 threads lower and work a row of stitches over 4 threads, between the stitches of the first row.

Slanted bricking

This stitch is also worked in interlocking rows, but over 2 vertical and 4 horizontal threads which gives a smooth, slanted texture.

Parisian stitch

This is a small, close, filling stitch worked in interlocking rows, over 1 and then over 3 horizontal threads.

Hungarian stitch

Again, this stitch is worked in interlocking rows, over 2 and then 4 horizontal threads.

Knot stitch

This slanting stitch is worked over 3 threads of canvas and caught down with a small slanting stitch across the center of the stitch. The rows are interlocking.

Knot stitch : working the second stage

Romanian or Roman stitch

This stitch consists of 2 rows linked with a row of stitches worked in a similar way to outline stitch. Work from left to right, and work each stitch from the top down over 6 threads and then work the central crossbar over the stitch working from right to left, one hole on each side of the long stitch. Complete the row in this manner.

Romanian or Roman stitch 2

The 2nd row is worked in the same way. To complete the stitch, a dividing row of outline stitch is worked from right to left, moving one hole to the left and two back all the way. This dividing row can be worked in the same color as the main stitch, or in a contrasting color

or yarn. On double weave canvas it creates an extremely pretty effect to work the main stitch over narrow strips of ribbon.

Romanian or Roman stitch, stage 1

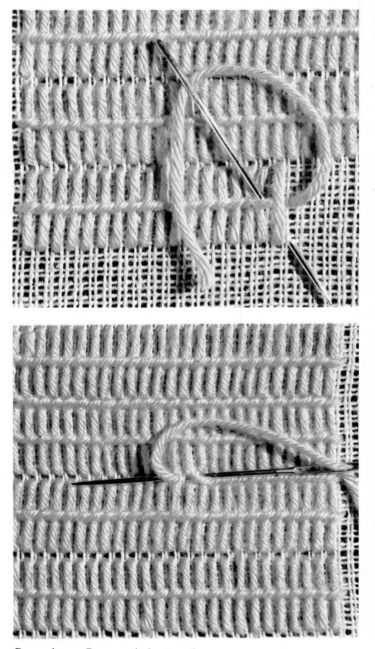

Romanian or Roman stitch, stage 2

Roman Bricking

This is an interesting variation of Romanian or Roman stitch which gives a rich braiding effect.

Work in the same manner as Romanian stitch but going from right to left and taking the crossbar from left to right.

The second row is worked in the same way, from right to left, but interlocking the stitches by bringing out the first stitch from behind the same hole as the crossing stitch of the previous row.

This may seem a little complicated at first but the illustration should help. This stitch gives a decorative effect well worth adding to your stitch library.

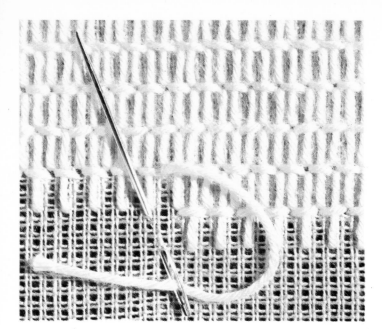

Roman bricking

French stitch

This very closely textured stitch is worked in diagonal rows from top left to bottom right. It makes a most attractive pattern for a background or for incorporating in a design.

Work the main stitch from the bottom up over 4 threads then a central crossbar over it from right to left. Repeat the long stitch in the same holes and then work the crossbar from left to right, starting from the same hole as the previous crossbar.

Move 4 holes down to start the next stitch.

French stitch

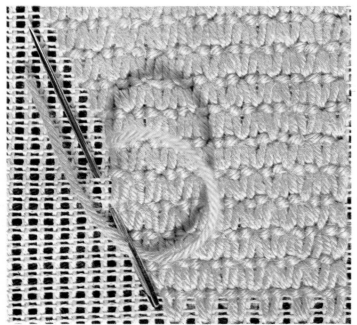

Fern stitch

This stitch is worked downward in vertical rows.

Start from the top left of the work. Insert the needle 2 holes down and 2 across and come out again one hole to the left. Insert the needle 2 holes up and 2 across and

come out again one hole below the starting point of the previous stitch.

Continue down the length of the row and work the next one immediately alongside.

Fern stitch

Rococo stitch

This stitch gives an attractive star-like pattern and makes a good background stitch. Work as for Romanian stitch working either 3 or 4 long stitches all from the same holes but held apart by the crossbars as shown in the picture. To start the 2nd stitch bring the needle out 4 holes along from the starting point of the first stitch and fit the second row in between the sections of the first row.

This stitch can be seen in the Harvest Fields sampler incorporated into the background area. You will find that this is a very useful stitch for adding texture and interest to the background of charted pictures.

Rococo stitch

Satin
stitches

As its name suggests, satin stitch is smooth and flat. On a large piece of canvas work it is enhanced by working rough textured stitches around it such as long-legged cross-stitch. When combined with other stitches such as tent stitches or when worked to form brocade-like textures, different stitches are formed, for instance Byzantine, checker, cushion, Florentine, Jacquard, Milanese and Moorish stitches.

It is shown in several variations in this chapter, beginning with the simple but very effective square shape of cushion stitch. See how entirely different it looks worked into a zigzag, or into a square of 4 concentric triangles for a diamond. This last version makes a lovely stylized flower head.

Diagonal rows of satin stitch made interesting by using different colors

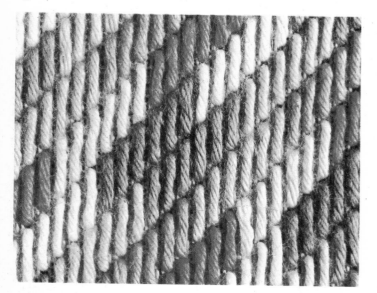

Satin stitch

The panel shows how the stitch is constructed while the illustration shows how it looks as a block of complete stitches.

Since satin stitch is quite long, crossing 2 or even 3 or more threads, it is not a good choice for pillows or chair covers because surfaces may catch or pull. When working with the family of satin stitches, make sure that the threads cover the canvas well, adding more strands of yarn if necessary. When using more than one strand pull them all gently to insure an even finish.

Cushion stitch

Before you begin working the plump squares of this stitch, decide carefully, which way it is going to lie in the diagonal, its direction will make all the difference to the overall effect. The diagrams show both a checkered

How satin stitch is constructed

effect and a diamond effect. The diagram shows a way of padding to fill the center gap.

Work each square in the order shown, working the diagonal stitch AB before working sections 3 and 4.

Half cushion stitch

This is cushion stitch worked over as many threads as required until it leaves the neat triangular shape of half a square. These can be built up into diamonds.

Diagonal satin stitch

Diagonal satin stitch worked in bands over 2 threads. This stitch can be worked in alternative directions and over a different number of threads to give interesting zigzag effects. On the right of the illustration is shown diagonal satin stitch worked over 4 and 4 threads. on the left over 2 and 4.

Padded satin stitch

The area to be covered is first trammed and then stitched over to give a well defined padded effect.

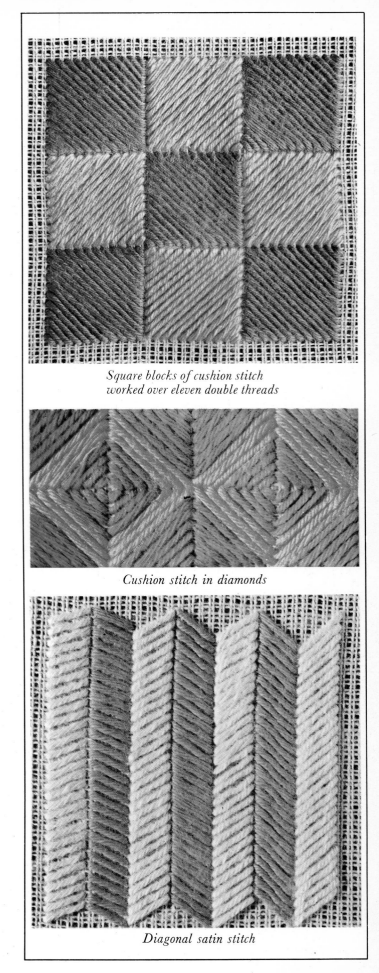

Square blocks of cushion stitch worked over eleven double threads

Cushion stitch in diamonds

Diagonal satin stitch

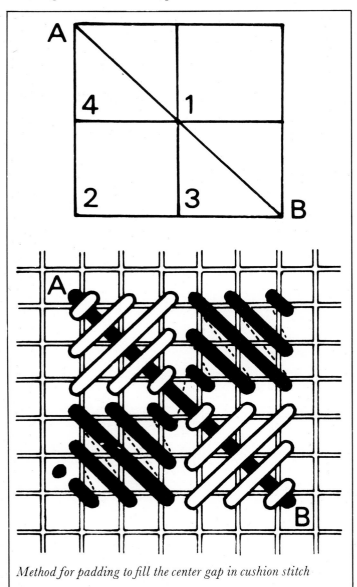

Method for padding to fill the center gap in cushion stitch

Needlepoint know-how

Practice stitches in a sampler

The early English samplers which were made from the fifteenth to the eighteenth century are fascinating works of art, but in early Victorian days their style became rather uniform and dull. Most of them were worked entirely in cross-stitch or tent stitch, using wool or silk yarns. The designs consisted mainly of the alphabet, the maker's name, her age and the date. Later they became more interesting and elaborate, frequently showing family pets and hobbies.

Modern samplers too, have progressed from the dull style of the Victorian days as shown by the exciting sampler which we illustrate, which is an adventure in color, texture and pattern. It could be used most effectively as a wall panel but also looks marvelous as a pillow or tote bag. It is essential with needlepoint to have a good practice ground for each new stitch that you learn, and it is a good idea to work two samplers at the same time, one as a practice ground and one for a clear example of each stitch.

About 1 inch of the Harvest Fields sampler we show is missing from the right side of the picture, but the complete design is shown in the diagram.

Make a plan of action

Before beginning to make a sampler, decide on a basic plan of the design and color scheme you will use.

If this is your first attempt, you may like to copy the Harvest Fields sampler. You may on the other hand prefer to create your own design but, unless you are experienced, try to avoid difficult curves by planning a geometric design.

Copying the design

The chart on the right shows the Harvest Fields design reduced to one third of its actual size. All you have to do is copy the chart, multiplying the measurements by three, onto a larger sheet of graph or plain paper.

Place the copied design securely underneath the canvas, and trace in the lines using a ruler and a ball point pen with waterproof ink.

This sampler is worked on single thread canvas with 18 threads to 1 inch. Make sure when you buy the canvas that it is at least 3 inches larger than the design all around. You can use any type of canvas as long as you choose the one most appropriate to the design—coarse canvas for large shapes, and fine canvas for smaller, more intricate ones. A frame is not really necessary for working samplers of this size. Do remember that yarns give texture as well as color, so that it is wise not to use too many colors or the effect will be muddled. Also make sure you use enough strands of yarn on the needle because the stitches must cover the canvas fully. Always

Harvest Fields sampler

keep tension perfectly even so that design is not distorted.

Yarns and colors

The list gives the complete range of yarns for the sampler, but if you are planning your own design you can experiment with unusual yarns as much as you like. Mix silks with wool or try a fluffy textured wool with the smooth texture of raffia—or make it more exciting with a border of ribbons or beads.

Go to town on texture

One stitch pattern for the Harvest Fields sampler is suggested in the diagram, but of course you may want to plan your own. Each stitch pattern gives a different texture, so when making a sampler, be sure to arrange the textures in a balanced composition. Mix them well, and avoid using all the smooth textures on the one side and all the rough ones on the other.

		greens	yellows	oranges
DMC	Matania	2218 (1)	2307 (2)	
DMC	6 stranded embroidery floss	471 (1)	444 (2)	783 (1)
DMC	tapestry wool	7549 (9)		
		7355 (4)		
		7353 (7)		
		7359 (4)		
DMC Floralia			7455 (12)	7437 (12)

(numbers in brackets = skeins)

You will also need one ball of tweed-texture knitting wool and a skein of cocoa-colored plasticized raffia.

Area shown opposite

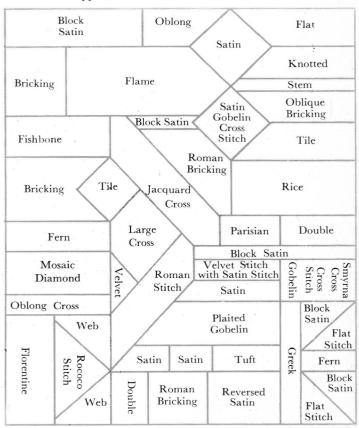

Cats in needlepoint

Louis J. Gartner, who designed and executed these realistic looking pieces of needlepoint, makes up his designs by 'borrowing' the elements, sometimes from magazine and book illustrations.

The leopard cub was taken from a magazine illustration and enlarged life size to fit into a 14 inch diameter circle. The original picture was full of small detail which decided the designer to work the animal itself in petit point against a gros point background. To reproduce the plump roundness of a live animal and the subtlety of the baby fur, Louis J. Gartner used twelve different "fur" colored yarns plus black and white. The shaded background to the animal was achieved by working colors in slanting stripes, so that the tones blended imperceptibly, giving an effect of space behind the cub.

With a little practice and imagination it is possible to reproduce almost anything in this way making use of the stitches in your stitch library. The delightful thing about needlepoint is that it is adaptable and easy to work, and the pieces you produce which are all your own are those which will give the greatest satisfaction, and may become the collector's pieces of tomorrow.

This tiger's head was designed and executed by Louis J. Gartner. The design was "borrowed" from an album jacket design.

Covering a footstool in canvas

If a favorite stool shows signs of wear on the top fabric, it is relatively simple to work a new top in needlepoint to re-cover it. The stitches used in the design shown here suggest stripes. The stitches chosen are chain stitch method 1, chain stitch method 2 and plaited Gobelin and some stem stitch (see diagrams). Canvas work is particularly suitable for footstool tops because it is so hard wearing. For the best results the important thing to bear in mind is always to use the best quality yarns and canvas. Also, special care must be taken when planning the design as this must view equally well from every angle.

For the footstool top
You will need
☐ Canvas (to assess amount required measure across the width of the stool plus the drop on both sides. Measure in the same way for the length and add 6 inches to each measurement to allow for blocking)
☐ Muslin of a similar amount
☐ Soft lead pencil
☐ Dressmaking pins
☐ Tapestry yarn or crewel wool in the amounts specified for the design chosen
☐ Tapestry needle No 18
☐ Fine ½ inch upholstery tacks for corners
☐ Brass headed upholstery tacks (sufficient to go around the stool placed close together)

Before you begin
Remove the old covering and make sure that the existing padding is firm and even. If not, the top should be re-upholstered.

Making a pattern
Working out the shape of the pattern is first done with muslin, just like a toile in dressmaking. The muslin must be big enough to more than cover the seat area and the drop. Use a soft pencil, and mark a vertical and a horizontal line from side to side across the center of the muslin, using the thread of the weave as a guide. Draw a similar line vertically in the center of the stool. Position the muslin on the stool, matching the lines. Pin the muslin to the stool top, starting at the center of the crossed lines and working out simultaneously to all four sides, placing the pins at 3 inch intervals. Continue these lines of pins down the depth of the drop. Pin the corners to make miters. With a soft pencil, mark the area of the top of the stool, the edge of the frame and both sides of each mitered corner. Take the muslin off the stool and measure the length and width of the muslin to make sure that it corresponds exactly to the measurements of the stool. If it does not, the muslin has been pulled out of shape. Working on a firm surface, pin the muslin onto brown paper, making sure that the weave of the muslin is straight. The pattern on the muslin may be slightly irregular but make

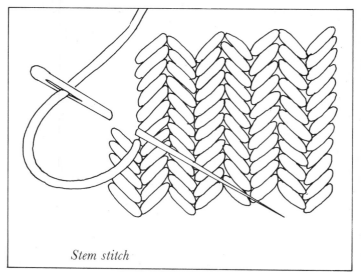

Stem stitch

the brown paper absolutely symmetrical. Mark the vertical and horizontal lines on the canvas to match up with those on the paper pattern. Pin the pattern to the canvas and mark with a felt pen around the edge. This gives the area of the canvas to be worked. Cut the canvas to a square leaving at least 3 inches margin all around for blocking.

Covering the stool
When you have completed working the design on the canvas for the stool cover, block and trim the work, leaving the unworked areas of canvas in the corners for mitering. Turn the seam allowances to the back of the

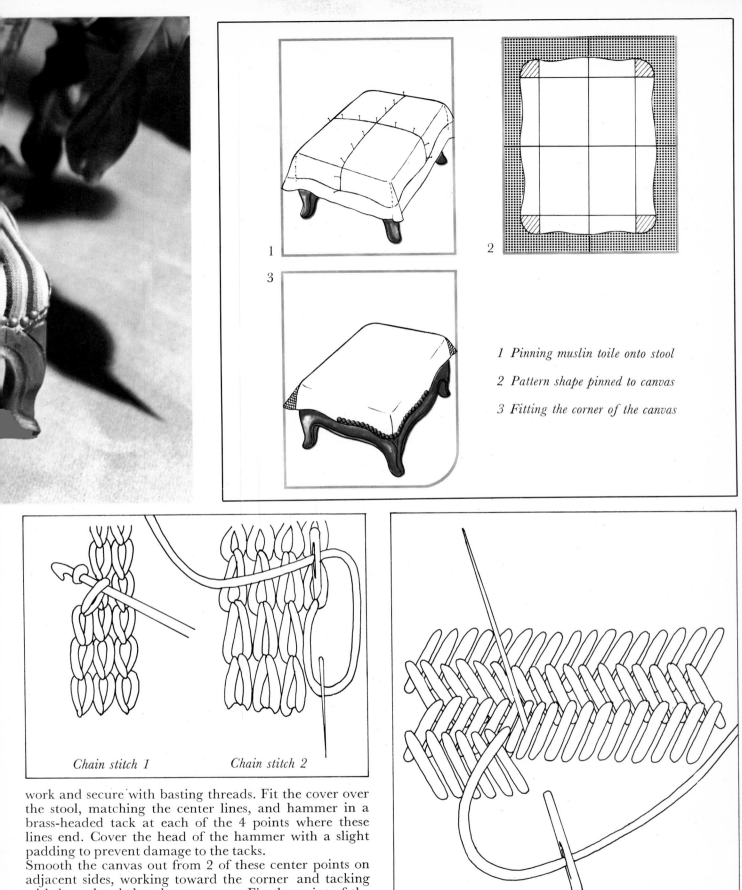

1 Pinning muslin toile onto stool

2 Pattern shape pinned to canvas

3 Fitting the corner of the canvas

Chain stitch 1   *Chain stitch 2*

Plaited Gobelin stitch

work and secure with basting threads. Fit the cover over the stool, matching the center lines, and hammer in a brass-headed tack at each of the 4 points where these lines end. Cover the head of the hammer with a slight padding to prevent damage to the tacks.

Smooth the canvas out from 2 of these center points on adjacent sides, working toward the corner and tacking with brass-headed tacks as you go. Fix the point of the canvas corner to the stool using an upholstery tack then ease the edges of the worked canvas together to meet at the corner edge (see diagram).

Work the remaining corners in the same way, working the diagonally opposite corner next.

Belts made with cross stitch

Despite its simplicity, cross-stitch can be extremely effective and adaptable. These patterns for example, make marvelous belts and borders. It is fascinating to experiment with color schemes because a design originally in one color combination will look entirely different in another.

For the belts
You will need
To obtain a design about $\frac{2}{3}$ of the size of the motifs illustrated, use double thread canvas with 14 threads to the inch and tapestry wool, 6-strand floss or a matte embroidery cotton. You can adapt designs to coarser or finer canvas, using appropriately thicker or finer yarns.

Orange and brown design
This is a simple pattern using square motifs in 3 colors. Try using 3 tones of one color or, for a checkerboard effect, use a black background with gray and white centers. For an all over design, the square motifs could be grouped to form geometric designs and with an interesting use of color against a contrasting background shade, a fascinating patchwork effect can be achieved.

Orange and brown design

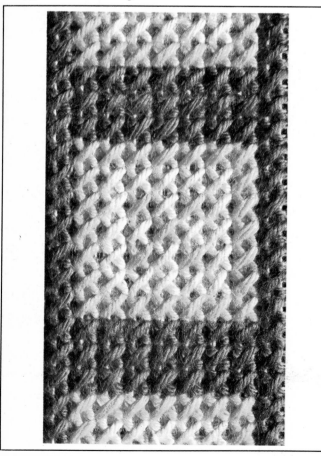

Red and gold design
This motif lends itself to being repeated over a large area and readily adapts itself for a cummerbund, bag, footstool top, cushion or chair seat. Or make an exotic vest in gold, copper and silver metallic yarns.

Red and gold design

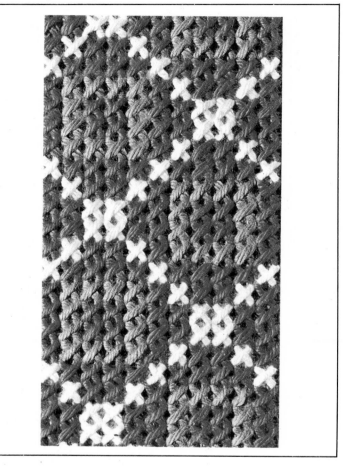

Pink with green shamrocks
Use half cross-stitch or tent stitch for this pretty design. If you make this up in a different combination of colors, the whole character of the design becomes more sophisti-

Pink with green shamrocks

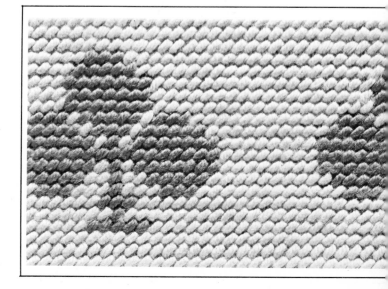

cated. To add more texture, you could work either the background or the shamrocks in tiny cross-stitch, or tram the shamrocks to give a raised effect.

Blue and brown design

This L-shaped repeat motif is worked in upright Gobelin stitch worked over 4, 3 and 2 double threads of canvas. The background is worked over 1 thread. A three-dimensional effect is obtained by using tones of one color for the L-shape. This motif can be adapted to build up geometric designs.

Blue and brown design

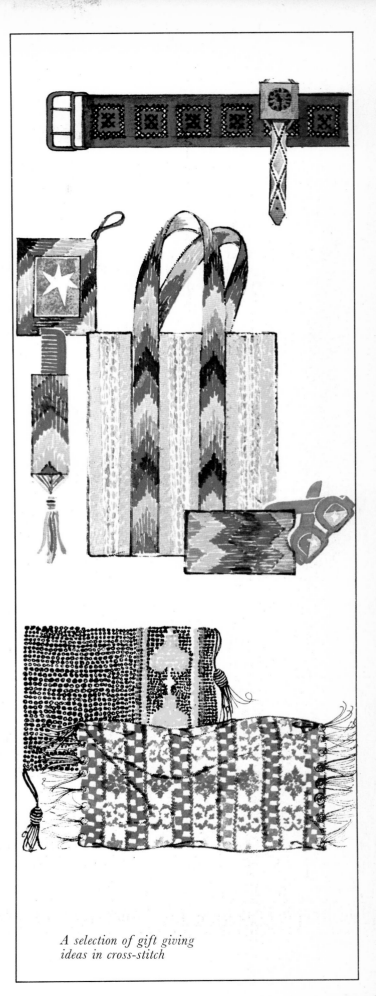

A selection of gift giving ideas in cross-stitch

Follow the band

Needlepoint has recently been updated by working it in brilliant colors for fashion accessories. The belts and bands given here are worked on double thread canvas with ten double threads to 1 inch.

Tent stitch is used throughout. All colors refer to tapestry yarn.

For the neckband
Finished size — 2 inches wide by neck measurement

You will need
☐ Canvas 6 inches by 22 inches
☐ ½ yard ribbon, 2 inches wide
☐ 24 inches leather thonging
☐ 2 small skeins each of red, purple, black, orange, yellow and lilac which is shown on the chart as white for clarity

Method of working
Work the design from the chart for the required length. Block and trim the canvas. Turn the raw canvas on the long sides to the back of the work and catch them down with herringbone stitch. To make the channel through which the thonging slots, turn the raw canvas on the two ends to the back of the work and back stitch them down ⅜ inch from the edge. Line the band with ribbon using slip stitches and working through only one thickness of canvas at the ends so that the thonging channel is left open.

Slot the thonging upward through one channel and downward through the other (see illustration).

For the fringed girdle
Finished size — 2 inches wide by the waist measurement, taken loosely plus 6½ inches overlap. (For a wider belt use coarser canvas)

You will need
☐ Canvas 7 inches by 36 inches
☐ Lining 4 inches by 36 inches
☐ 6 small skeins each of red, lilac; 3 small skeins each of purple, yellow; 2 small skeins each of black and orange
☐ Piece of cardboard 3¼ inches by 6 inches
☐ Large snap fasteners

Method of working
Work the design from the chart for the required length. Block and trim the canvas. Fold under the raw canvas and herringbone stitch into place. To make the fringe wind yarn for 3 inches along the cardboard. Carefully sew one end of the loops to the canvas ¼ inch in from the end of the girdle, making sure that every strand is included. Slide the cardboard out and work a row of back stitches to secure the fringe. Complete work by lining the girdle, enclosing the ends of the fringe. Use snaps for fastening, laying one end of the girdle over the other (see illustration).

For the thonged belt
Finished size — 2½ inches wide by the waist measurement, loosely taken

You will need
☐ Canvas 6½ inches by 36 inches
☐ Lining 4 inches by 36 inches
☐ 45 inches leather thonging
☐ 10 eyelets and eyelet tool
☐ 4 small skeins orange; 3 small skeins red; 7 small skeins lilac

Method of working
Work the design from the chart for the required length. Block and trim the canvas. Fold under the raw canvas and herringbone stitch into place. Line the belt and then insert five eyelets vertically, evenly spaced on each end of the belt. Lace the thonging through and tie.

A belt with leather thonging laces and a detail of thonging

The neckband with leather thonging tie

For the wristband
Finished size —2 inches deep by wrist measurement

You will need
☐ Canvas 6 inches by 10 inches
☐ ¼ yard ribbon, 2 inches wide
☐ 24 inches leather thonging
☐ 1 small skein each of the colors given for the neckband

Method of working
Work the same way and to the same design as for the neckband.

Wristband to match the neckband and girdle

A fringed girdle to wear with a simple dress

Chart for matching wristband, neckband and fringed girdle

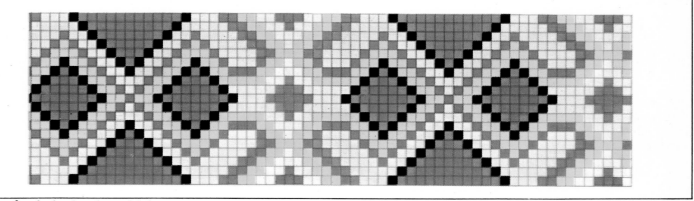

Chart for the leather thonged belt

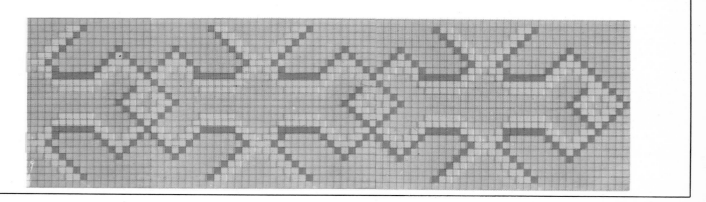

Make a lighter or glasses case

If you are not yet very experienced at needlepoint you will find that both lighter and glasses cases are quick, fun and easy to make.

You can try out your favorite stitch to work an all-over, rich textured pattern, or you can use any of the other stitches you have learned.

For the glasses case
You will need
☐ Canvas
☐ Yarn
☐ 4 inch length of cord
☐ Lining

Method of working
Cut the canvas to measure $18\frac{1}{2}$ inches by $6\frac{3}{4}$ inches, and cover an area which measures $14\frac{1}{2}$ inches by $2\frac{3}{4}$ inches with stitches.

Block and trim the canvas, then cut a piece of lining material to the trimmed size. To prepare the needlepoint for seaming, fold crosswise leaving $2\frac{1}{2}$ inch flap, wrong sides facing.

Stitch the piece of cord securely to the seam allowance on the right side, 1 inch down from the opening. Baste edges and seam.

With right sides of the lining together, turn up $6\frac{3}{8}$ inches leaving a $2\frac{7}{8}$ inch flap. Stitch the side seams from the fold to within $\frac{3}{8}$ inch of the opening. Fold the seam allowance around the flap and across the opening to the wrong side of the lining, baste and press. Slip the lining into the case, using a blunt pencil to push it right down into the corners. Pin the lining around the edges of the opening and flap, matching the seams of the lining to the seams of the case, and baste them together and slip stitch neatly into place. Remove basting. Fold over the $2\frac{1}{2}$ inch flap and tuck it under the cord.

For the lighter case
You will need
☐ Canvas
☐ Yarn
☐ Lining

Method of working
For an average size lighter case, cut the canvas to measure $6\frac{3}{4}$ inches by 10 inches and embroider an area measuring $2\frac{3}{4}$ inches by 6 inches. Block the canvas and prepare it for seaming. With the right side of the work facing you, fold it in half and stitch the side seams, finishing as described for the glasses case, omitting the flap and cord.

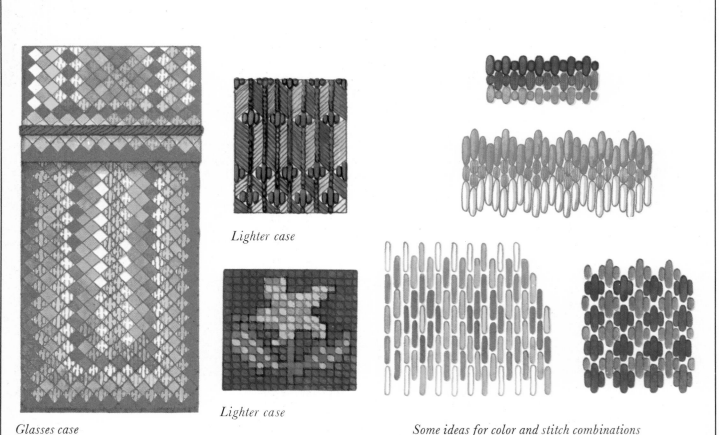

Glasses case

Lighter case

Lighter case

Some ideas for color and stitch combinations

A simple wild pansy purse worked in three stitches

More small gifts to make

Many people who might be tempted to try their hand at needlepoint are daunted by the large pieces of work they see in stores and magazines. Although these large pieces can provide inspiration, the inexperienced embroiderer needs encouragement in the form of smaller simple pieces. These should be well designed and colorful enough to be fun to make and pleasing to give.

Any of the needlepoint articles shown here should be simple enough to be worked by someone new to this form of embroidery—or might be worked just as effectively in more complex stitches by the experienced embroiderer.

A tiny wild pansy inspired the motif for the change purse in needlework and the glasses case is based upon an abstract form of the same shape. The design for the purse has been kept very simple and all unnecessary detail omitted. The central motif is outlined with a waterproof felt tipped pen and traced through onto the canvas. The natural colors of the flower are worked in three stitches:

tent stitch for the outline of the design, small diagonal satin stitch for the flower and mosaic stitch.

The flower shape has been further simplified for the glasses case and the resulting design is more stylized. The central figures are worked in cross-stitch, and cushion stitch is used for the background. When the stitchery has been completed, stretch the canvas over a thin piece of cardboard cut to the shape required, glueing the turnings to the reverse side for the lining of the glasses case.

The design can be repeated on the reverse side of the case, or the reverse side can be worked in cushion stitch in just one toning color. After stitching the two sides of the glasses case together, cover the join with velvet ribbon or cord. Or, work an edge stitch around each piece of canvas, then stitch the two sides together. The tiny lighter case is a simple rectangular strip of canvas worked in a variation of bricking stitch, folded in half and sewn up along the sides. An edge stitch finishes off the piece along the folded edges.

Making a pincushion

1. Choose a simple motif or design for a square or rectangular pincushion and make a chart on graph paper before beginning to work.
Each small square on the chart represents one stitch.

A combination of stitches will provide a pleasing contrast in texture. For instance tent, Gobelin, straight and satin stitches are all smooth. Cross stitches, rice and star are all semi-rough. Double cross, oblong and tufted stitches are very rough. Remember that strong texture is often most effective when used in small areas.

2. A monogram or single letter is easy to work out on a chart, and makes a particularly appealing pincushion. The letter or letters might be worked in tent stitch and the background in cushion stitch or alternating rows of tent stitch and long-legged cross-stitch. Use Anchor Tapisserie wools and work on single-weave canvas with 14 threads to 1 inch, using a No 20 tapestry needle.

3. After the design has been worked, block the canvas and trim off the excess, allowing $\frac{5}{8}$ inch turnings. For the backing, cut a square or rectangle of velvet or other sturdy fabric to the size of the trimmed canvas. Baste the turnings to the wrong side to make a neat, accurate square or rectangle. Baste the canvas turnings to the back of the work and pin the velvet to the canvas, wrong sides together. Hem the velvet firmly into place, stitching into the outer row of needlepoint stitches. Leave half of one side open for stuffing. Bran, lambswool and emery powder are all suitable materials for stuffing and should be packed very tightly. Close the opening with pins and sew closely when fully stuffed. Make neat by sewing cord all around the edge, covering seam.

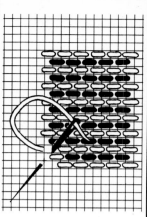

A variation of bricking stitch ; each stitch is worked over two threads

△ *A single stitch is used for this tiny lighter case*

◁ *Rich colors and an elegant design for glasses case*

▽ *Other gift-giving ideas in needlepoint*

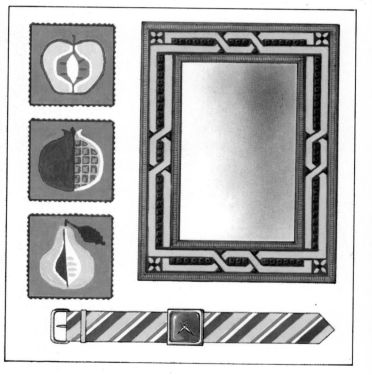

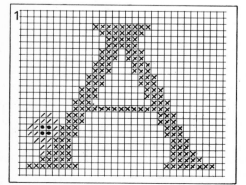

1

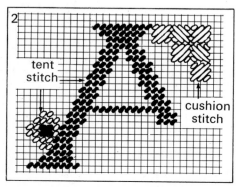

2

tent stitch

cushion stitch

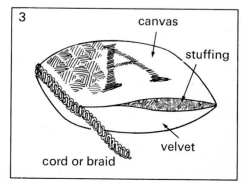

3

canvas

stuffing

velvet

cord or braid

50

Smart specs

These smart and distinctive cases are both quick and easy to work and make ideal gifts or bazaar items. Made up in two attractive designs, both cases are lined with a contrasting fabric. The lining gives protection to the glasses and a professional finish to the work.

For the Zebra-striped case
approx 3½ inches by 6½ inches

You will need
- ☐ ¼ yard single canvas, 10 threads to 1 inch
- ☐ White and black rug wool
- ☐ ⅛ yard fabric for lining
- ☐ ¾ yard black cord

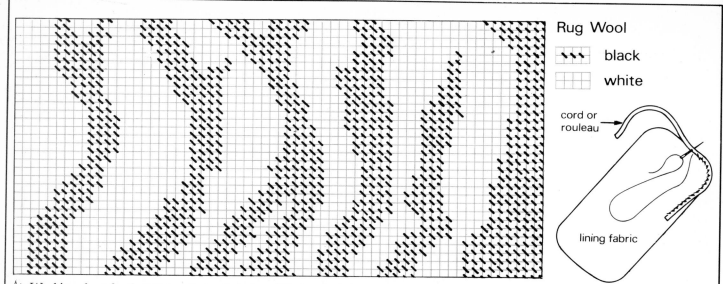

Rug Wool

ᐳᐳᐳ black

□ white

△△ *Working chart for the "Zebra Stripes" design. Work entirely in tent stitch over one thread*

cord or rouleau →

lining fabric

△ *A short length of cord or rouleau covers the join at one end of the first side of the case*

▽ *Working chart for the "Roman Stripes" design. Areas of tent stitch are worked over one thread and mosaic stitch over one and two threads*

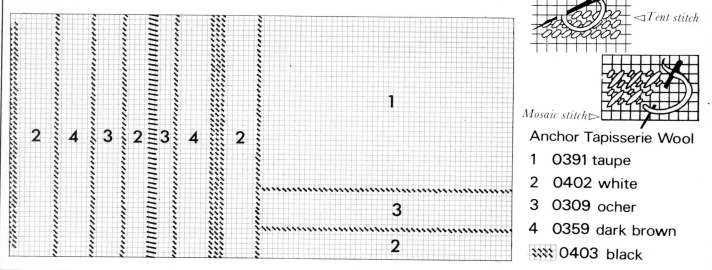

◁*Tent stitch*

Mosaic stitch▷

Anchor Tapisserie Wool
1 0391 taupe
2 0402 white
3 0309 ocher
4 0359 dark brown
▧▧ 0403 black

For the Roman striped case
approx 3 inches by 6 inches

You will need
□ ¼ yard single canvas, 16 threads to 1 inch
□ Anchor Tapisserie Wool in the following colors: 0391 taupe, 0402 white, 0403 black, 0309 ocher, 0359 dark brown
□ ⅛ yard contrasting fabric for lining
□ ¾ yard black cord or rouleau
□ ⅛ yard Pellon

Method of working
Trace the outline of the case onto the canvas twice, allowing at least 1 inch of canvas all around for making up. Follow the stitch chart for the design required, working the design twice, for the front and the back of the case. If desired, one side of the case can be made up from suede, or some other sturdy fabric.

Making up the case
Trace off the outline of the case onto the wrong side of the fabric of the lining twice. Allow ¾ inch turning all around and trim away excess fabric.
Trim the canvas to within ¾ inch of the worked area and snip at the corners.
Press under the turnings of both the lining and the canvas, place the wrong sides together and pin. Insert a layer of Pellon if required. Whip stitch the two layers together around all the edges.
Slip stitch a short piece of cord or rouleau along one end of the first side of the case covering the join. Make the ends neat by slipping them into the seam as shown in the diagram. Repeat the procedure for making up the second side of the case, pressing together under the turnings and stitching together the lining fabric and the canvas. To complete the case, whip stitch the two sides of the case together and cover the join with another piece of cord or rouleau, hiding the ends as before.
The cases are made up in tent stitch and Mosaic stitch.

A pincushion for the apple of your eye

A pin cushion is a good way to begin working from a charted design. This is less expensive than buying a painted or trammed canvas, which will confine you to the most commercially available designs, while a charted picture gives you the opportunity of picking your own colors and building up your own designs. For instance, you can repeat the apple motif given below at random all over a pillow or turn it into a yellow Golden Delicious or a green Granny Smith.

Apple pincushion

This plump apple pincushion uses lustrous cushion stitch to interpret the shiny apple, rough reinforced cross-stitch

Two pincushions to work: one from the chart below, one row by row

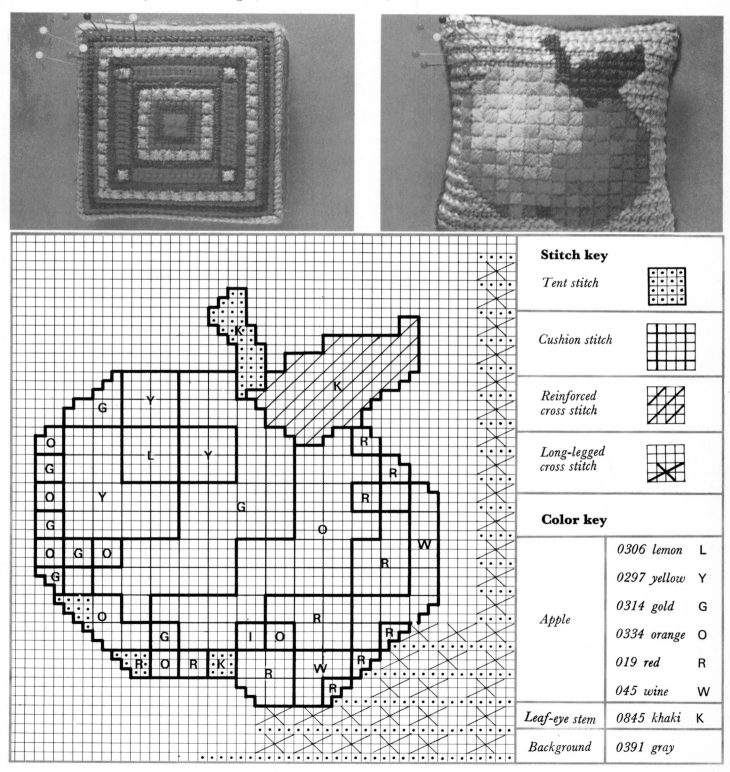

Stitch key

Tent stitch	
Cushion stitch	
Reinforced cross stitch	
Long-legged cross stitch	

Color key

Apple	0306 lemon	L
	0297 yellow	Y
	0314 gold	G
	0334 orange	O
	019 red	R
	045 wine	W
Leaf-eye stem	0845 khaki	K
Background	0391 gray	

for the gnarled leaf, and precise tent stitch for the neat shape of the stem and eye.

For the apple pincushion
You will need
☐ Single-weave canvas 10 inches by 10 inches, 14 threads to 1 inch. (Finished size about 4 inches square.)
☐ No 20 tapestry needle and a sharp needle for sewing up
☐ Velvet or other backing material 6 inches by 6 inches. One skein each of Anchor Tapisserie wools 0306, 0297, 0314, 0334, 019, 045, 0845; and 2 skeins of 0391
☐ 18 inches of cord for trimming
☐ For filling, sawdust from the lumber yard

Method of working
Prevent the canvas from fraying by binding the edges with masking tape. On the chart each square represents 1 canvas thread crossing which is to be covered by a single tent stitch.
Apple: Work in cushion stitch in groups of 4, over 3 threads.
Eye and Stem: work in tent stitch over 1 thread.
Leaf: Work in reinforced cross-stitch (i.e. cross-stitch worked twice over) over 2 threads. This insures that there is a good coverage of the canvas.
Background: Work in alternate rows of long-legged cross-stitch worked over 2 threads, and tent stitch worked over 1 thread.
NB To clarify chart, background symbols do not cover entire area.

Blocking the canvas back in shape
When the design is completed block the canvas and trim off excess canvas allowing $\frac{5}{8}$ inch turnings.

Finishing off
To back the cushion, cut a square of velvet to the size of the trimmed canvas. Baste the turnings to the wrong side to make a neat accurate square. Baste canvas turnings to back of work. Pin velvet to canvas, wrong sides together and whip the velvet firmly into place, stitching into the outer row of needlepoint stitches.
Leave center of one side open for stuffing.
Sawdust is the stuffing which best allows pins to be pushed in easily. Pack it in very tightly—a teaspoon will help. Close the opening with pins and whip tightly when fully stuffed. Brush off any sawdust left lying on the pincushion. Make neat by sewing cord all around edge.

Square pincushion
Method of working
The square pincushion is worked in delightful, bright, rich colors in a simple geometric design using a variety of lovely stitches. Work it outward from a center block of 4 cushion stitches in rows as follows: 2 rows tent stitch, 1 row cross-stitch, 1 row Smyrna cross-stitch, 1 row satin stitch, 1 row oblong cross-stitch with bars, 1 row long-legged cross-stitch, 1 row Smyrna cross-stitch, 1 row satin stitch, 1 row cross-stitch. For the sides work 1 row oblong cross-stitch with bars, 1 row long-legged cross-stitch, 1 row Smyrna cross-stitch, 1 row long-legged cross-stitch, 1 row oblong cross-stitch with bars. Work long-legged cross-stitch for seams.

Needlepoint cover story

Snap-on covers are just the thing to update a favorite clutch bag, either for day or evening wear. Cover the canvas with smooth satiny textures for smart occasions, rich, tweedy textures for country wear, or glittering gold or silver for evening wear. One basic bag can have a wardrobe of inter-changeable covers. Two interesting stitch combinations are given in this chapter.

For the needlepoint cover
You will need
☐ A plain clutch bag
☐ Sufficient canvas to cover the bag plus 2 inches extra all around for blocking and seam allowances

- [ ] Piece of lining the same size as the canvas
- [ ] 6 large snap fasteners
- [ ] Embroidery yarn
- [ ] Tapestry needle
- [ ] Heavy paper

Making the pattern

Measure the width of the bag and then measure the length from the front flap edge, up the front of the bag, over the top and down to the back edge. Draw a rectangle to these measurements on the paper and cut out the pattern of the outline.

Pin the pattern onto the canvas, making sure to follow the grain of the canvas. Mark the pattern outline with either basting stitches or a felt tipped pen. Find the canvas center by making two lines of basting stitches, one along the center lengthwise and the other across the center widthways.

Plan the design and stitches to be used

Method of working

Work the required area of stitching on the canvas, working out from the center as marked by the crossed lines of basting. When the embroidery is completed block the canvas. Trim the canvas to within $\frac{5}{8}$ inch of the stitching.

To make up

Cut the piece of lining the same size as the trimmed canvas. Fold the raw canvas seam allowance to the back of the work and baste in place. Turn $\frac{5}{8}$ inch to the wrong side of lining and press. Place the canvas and the lining wrong sides together and baste all around the edge. Stitch the two pieces together using a small slip

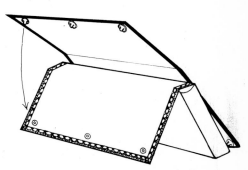

Sew snap fasteners on bag and cover

Half cushion stitch

A simple clutch bag glamorized with a snap-on needlepoint cover

stitch, remove basting.

Attach large snap fasteners, positioned as shown with one half of the snap on the bag and the other half on the underside of the cover.

Cushion stitch and cross-stitch

The stitches used for the bag cover illustrated are large cushion stitch and cross-stitch. The cushion stitch is made up of 15 stitches and the cross-stitch worked over 2 double threads of canvas each way. To prevent too long a stitch, work on either double thread canvas, with 15 double threads to the inch, or single thread canvas with 18 threads to the inch. For a more decorative finish the edge has been covered with narrow braid.

Cushion stitch and cross-stitch combine to make an interesting pattern

Algerian filling

This filling is made up of small blocks of satin stitch, in this case groups of 3 stitches worked over 4 double threads of canvas. The same stitch can be worked equally well on single thread canvas. It can either be worked entirely in one color to form a textured background or in complementary colors to form a pattern.

Algerian filling looks interesting when worked in a variety of colors

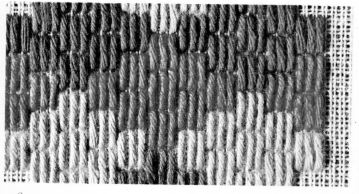

Needlepoint shoulder bag

This practical shoulder bag features an original needle-point panel in a bold geometric design, worked in subtle shades. Simple enough for a beginner to make, the needlepoint is backed with a sturdy fabric in a toning color.

For the bag
approx 10 inches square with 2 inch wide gusset and strap

You will need
☐ ½ yard by 23 inch wide single thread canvas, 18 threads to the inch
☐ Anchor Tapisserie Wool, 5 skeins 0280 muscat green; 4 skeins 0850 petrol blue; 3 skeins 0386 cream; 2 skeins each 0423 olive green and 0849 light petrol blue
☐ Tapestry frame
☐ Tapestry needle No 18
☐ 1 yard cotton twill, denim, canvas or similar fabric
☐ 1 yard lining fabric in a toning color
☐ 1 yard iron-on Pelomite
☐ Sewing thread to match fabric

Method of working
Mark the center of the canvas horizontally and vertically with a line of basting stitches and mount on the tapestry frame. The working chart gives the complete design with the bisecting lines indicated by arrows outside the design. These should coincide with the basting stitches.

The design is worked in cross-stitch, chain-stitch and petit point. Each square on the chart represents 2 threads of canvas and the stitch details indicate the number of threads over which each stitch is worked. Begin the work centrally and follow the key to determine which stitches and colors to use. If required, the worked canvas may be dampened, then pinned and blocked to the correct shape on a clean dry board, using rustproof thumb tacks. Leave the canvas to dry naturally for two to three weeks.

To make up the bag
Trim the canvas all around to within 1 inch of the worked area and miter the corners. Cut a square of fabric to match the size of the worked canvas, allowing ½ inch all around for turnings.

Cut the gusset (the base and sides) of the bag as one piece and cut a matching strip of fabric for the shoulder strap. This strip should measure 3 inches by approximately 32 inches, but adjust the length of the strap to fit.

Using the four components of the bag (front, back, gusset and strap) as patterns, cut matching pieces of lining fabric and iron-on Pelomite. Press the Pelomite to the back of each piece of fabric, first pressing back the turnings of the shoulder strap only. Do not apply Pelomite to the worked canvas yet.

With right sides together, machine stitch joining both ends of the long strips of fabric to form a ring. Before doing this, check the measurements once again to make certain that the two seams between the gusset and the shoulder strap will coincide exactly with the top edge of the worked canvas. Place the right side of the gusset against the worked surface of the canvas and machine stitch around three sides of the needlepoint design. This row of stitching should be 1 or 2 rows in from the edge to make certain that no exposed canvas appears. In order to stitch through the canvas smoothly, it is advisable to place a few sheets of tissue paper between the machine plate and the back of the canvas. Press back the inch of unworked canvas and place Pelomite (trimmed to exact

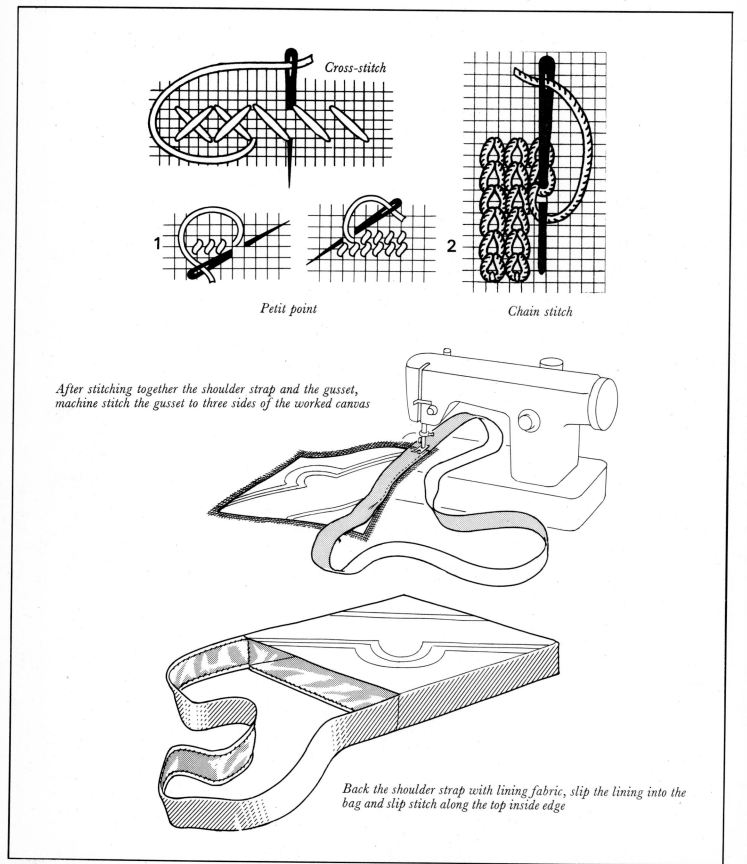

Cross-stitch

1

Petit point

2

Chain stitch

After stitching together the shoulder strap and the gusset, machine stitch the gusset to three sides of the worked canvas

Back the shoulder strap with lining fabric, slip the lining into the bag and slip stitch along the top inside edge

size of the worked area) over the back of the canvas covering the turnings. Iron on Pelomite. Press back the turnings along one side of the fabric back of the bag and machine stitch the gusset to this piece as before. Turn right side out.

Stitch together the front, back and gusset of the lining fabric with right sides together and press back the turnings. Baste the remaining strip of lining fabric to the inside of the shoulder strap and slip stitch along both sides. Slip the lining into the bag and slip stitch along the top edge.

To complete the bag, tuck the ends of the shoulder strap lining under the lining of the bag at each side and secure with slip stitch.

The working chart for the design. Each square represents two threads of the canvas

0849	⎫
0280	⎬ cross stitch
0423	⎭
0850	chain stitch
0386	petit point stitch

Anchor Tapisserie Wool

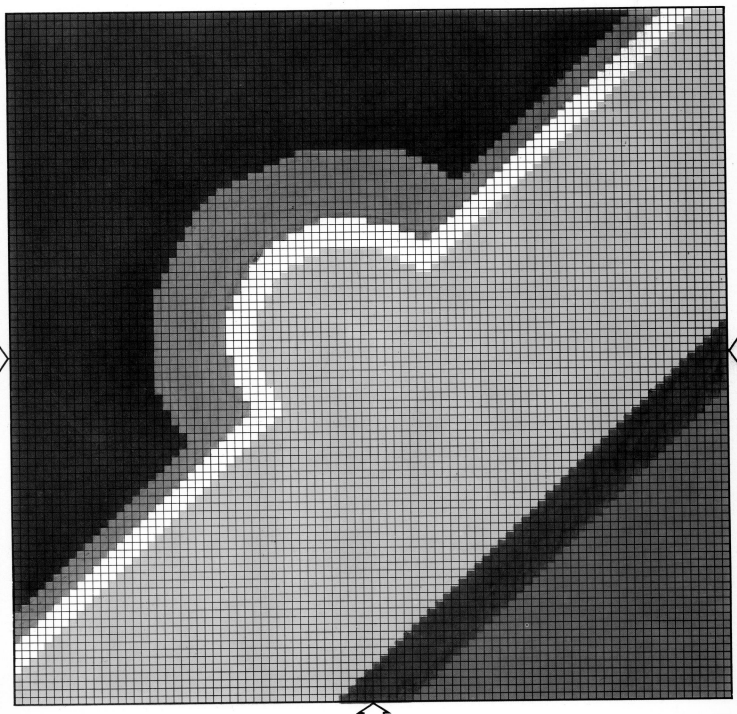

A beauty of a bag

Make no mistake about it, this is not just another shoulder bag! A roomy needlepoint "pouch" in rich colors combines a selection of not too difficult stitches with areas of padded leather, beads, tassels and macramé trim. The bag can be made on a more or less ambitious scale: work just one side of the canvas and the other in a complementary shade of burlap, or repeat the design on canvas for the second side. Either way, the result is a handsome—and useful—accessory.

For the bag
14½ inches by 12¾ inches
both sides worked on canvas

You will need
- ☐ ¾ yard single thread canvas, at least 18 inches wide (10 holes to the inch)
- ☐ Plain color fabric for lining
- ☐ 2 tapestry needles, large and medium
- ☐ Black thin-line marking pen
- ☐ Indelible thin-line marking pen in neutral color (ie medium gray)
- ☐ 1 large sheet of tracing paper
- ☐ Scraps of red leather
- ☐ Scraps of felt for padding leather .
- ☐ Polyester or nylon thread to match leather
- ☐ Wooden beads: large red, medium purple

Colors and quantities of yarns required for the bag
- ☐ 1 ounce sports yarn in each of the following colors: blue/mauve, deep blue, pink, warm pink, red, purple, dark blue/purple, dark red/purple, deep plum, tan
- ☐ 2 ounces knitting worsted (or substitute 3 strands of

Sports yarn) in each of the following colors: pink/mauve, blue/pink, deep pink, deep plum, red, tan, yellow, orange
- ☐ 1 ball Mercerized crochet Cotton, flesh
- ☐ 1 skein DMC Matania, buttercup 2444
- ☐ 5 skeins DMC 6-strand floss 816

Method of working
Work each side of the bag—or only one, if the other side is to be of burlap or another sturdy fabric—on a frame. If possible, work the entire side at once; or half of the canvas may be rolled up and tied to one side of the frame.

Transferring the design
Using the black marking pen, make a tracing of the entire design, repeating the panel with diamond shapes on the other side of the panel to include padded leather shapes. If just one side of the bag is to be worked on canvas, use only ½ yard of canvas and ½ yard of burlap; otherwise, repeat the design as a mirror image from the fold line.

Place the canvas over this tracing, mark out the design from the center hole with the neutral colored marking pen and count the threads in each panel. Note that the side panels have a center thread, and not a center hole. The diamonds in the side panels are on a true cross of the canvas, although they appear somewhat distorted because the holes are not square. Another point to consider is the differing angles of the diagonals in the piece; these are indicated on the working chart. Allow at least 1 inch turnings on all sides of the area to be worked.

The stitches to be used in each area are indicated on the working chart and stitch details are to act as a refresher for those unfamiliar or forgotten stitches.

Padded areas
The leather shapes are applied after all stitching on the canvas has been completed. Draw the shape to be padded onto felt scraps, then cut out the shape fractionally smaller all around. For more raised padding, consecutively smaller layers of felt are cut out. The smallest piece of padding is stitched to the canvas first and then each larger layer in turn, the stitches going right through to the background canvas (Figure 1). The leather shape is

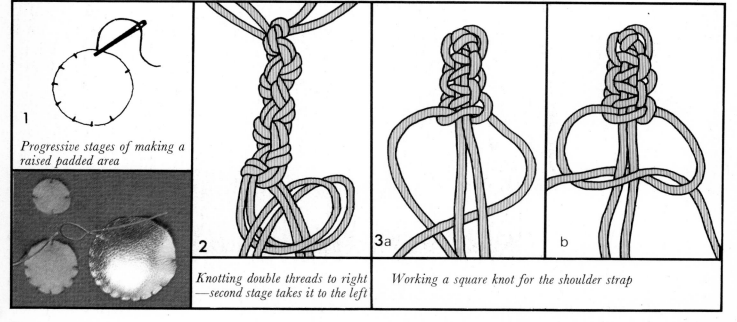

1 Progressive stages of making a raised padded area

2 Knotting double threads to right —second stage takes it to the left

3a **b** Working a square knot for the shoulder strap

then pinned over the padding and secured with three or four stitches around the edge or in the corners. Complete the stitching all around, using stab stitch and working the stitches at right angles to the cut edge. Stitches should extend from this edge into shape.

Finishing Touches

The border along the top of the bag is a double knotted chain in macrame worked with pink Sports yarn (figure 2). The shoulder strap is a square knot braid in macrame worked in knitting worsted in red and deep plum (figure 3). This braid should be long enough

to extend down both sides of the bag.

The large wool pompons and tassels are simply made from knitting worsted and, with wooden beads, strung along the lower edge of the bag. If both sides are in needlepoint, this edge will be a fold; if one side is fabric the lower edge will be a seam.

To line the bag, place the right sides of the lining fabric together and mark outline of the bag on one side. Machine or hand stitch just inside this line on three sides, leaving the top edge unstitched. Turn top edge over, slip the lining into the bag and slip stitch along the top edge.

Working chart for the shoulder bag. The panel with diamond shapes is repeated .

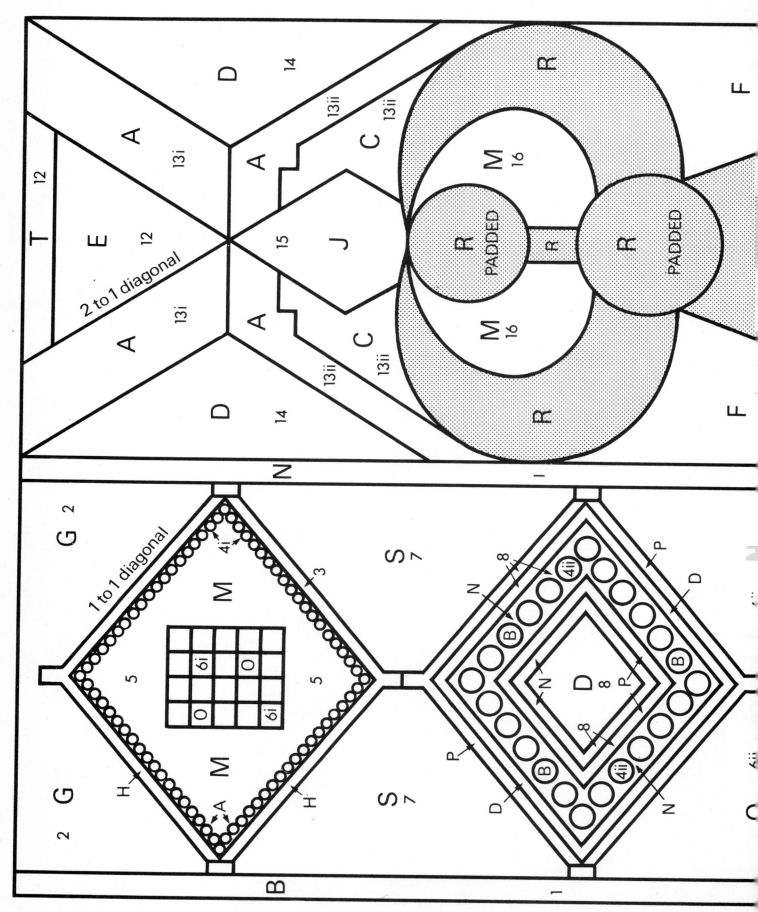

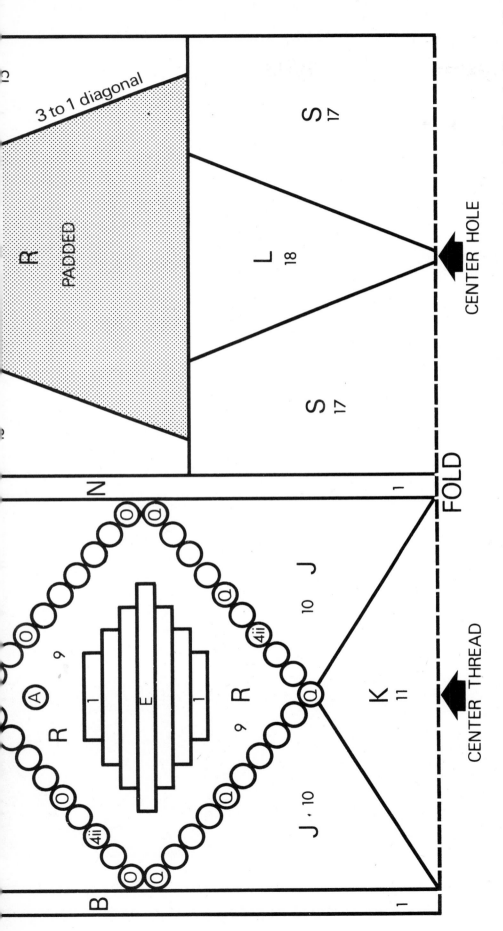

Key to stitches and materials

1. Raised chain band (knitting worsted)
2. Diagonal satin stitch worked over 2 threads in horizontal lines (knitting worsted)
3. Edging in vertical satin stitch worked over 4 holes (knitting worsted)
4i. French knots (sports yarn)
4ii. Large French knots (knitting worsted)
5. Tent stitch (Mercerized crochet cotton)
6i. Diagonal satin squares worked over 3 holes (Matania)
6ii. Same as 6i (sports yarn)
7. Parisian stitch worked over 1 and 3 threads (knitting worsted)
8. Same as 3 (sports yarn, double strand)
9. Same as 7, working each stitch in pairs (6-strand floss 3 strands)
10. Web stitch (sports yarn)
11. Same as 2, worked over 1 thread (sports yarn, double strand)
12. Same as 7 (knitting worsted)
13i. Cross-stitch worked over 1 hole (sports yarn)
13ii. Cross-stitch worked over 3 holes (sports yarn)
14. As 3, horizontal lines (knitting worsted)
15. Gobelin stitch worked over 5 holes (sports yarn, double strand)
16. Same as 6 (Mercerized crochet cotton)
17. Same as 2 (sports yarn)
18. Same as 3, worked in horizontal lines over 4 holes (sports yarn, double strand)

Key to colors

A Pink
B Deep pink
C Warm pink
D Orange
E Pink/mauve
F Deep blue
G Blue/mauve
H Blue/pink
J Purple
K Dark blue/purple
L Dark red/purple

M Flesh
N Tan
O Yellow
P Gold
Q Deep plum
R Dark red
S Red
T Violet

All aboard the petit-point express

Get up steam to make this delightfully original belt with its red locomotive and three carriages just about to pull into the little old-fashioned station. The belt is worked in petit point stitch and can be adjusted to fit most waist sizes.

For the belt
To fit a 26 inch to 28 inch waist

You will need
- [ ] Anchor Tapisserie Wool in the following colors and quantities: 1 skein each of 0335 red, 0398 gray, 0399 dark gray, 0298 yellow, 0245 dark green, 0268 leaf green, 0403 black, 0123 mauve, 0871 maroon, 0148 navy blue, 0146 bright blue, 0352 mid-brown, 0358 peat brown, 0380 dark brown, 0427 tan; approx 2 skeins of 0508 sky blue; approx 3 skeins of 0243 grass green
- [ ] 1 yard single thread canvas 16 holes to the inch, 23 inches wide
- [ ] 1 yard velvet for the lining
- [ ] 4 large snap fasteners

Method of working
The design is worked throughout in petit point stitch. Each row is worked so that it slopes in the opposite direction from the last, which prevents the canvas from warping.

The chart is divided into three sections—the engine, the caboose and one car, and the station. Beginning at the left-hand end of the canvas, work about 2 inches of plain grass and sky as shown at the front of the engine. Then work the engine following the chart and color key. Work the caboose and the mauve car next, joining them to the engine at the black link. Then work the

The engine, the tender and the three cars can be seen when the belt is laid out flat

maroon and navy blue cars in the same way. Add an area of plain grass and sky at the end as at the front of the engine. These plain sections can be lengthened as required to fit your waist measurement. Each square on the chart represents 4 stitches (2 horizontally by 2 vertically).

The station building is worked on a separate piece of canvas, as it forms the buckle of the belt.

To make up
When the embroidery is complete, trim the canvas to within ⅝ inch of the edge, and line both the belt and the station with the velvet. Sew a snap fastener to each corner of the velvet at the back of the station, and 2 to each end of the belt, adjusting the position as required.

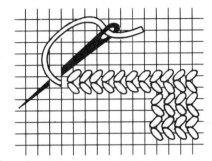

Petit point stitch in alternately sloping rows

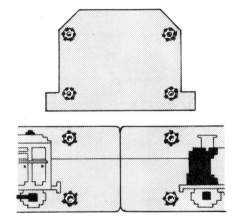

Sew a snap-fastener to each corner at the back of the station and two to each end of the belt

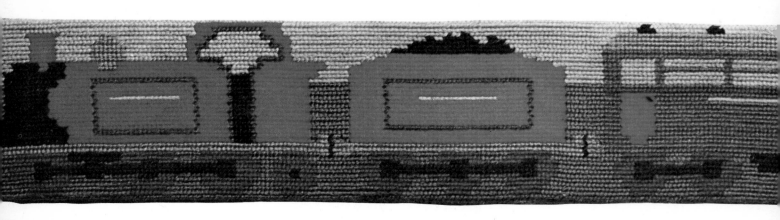

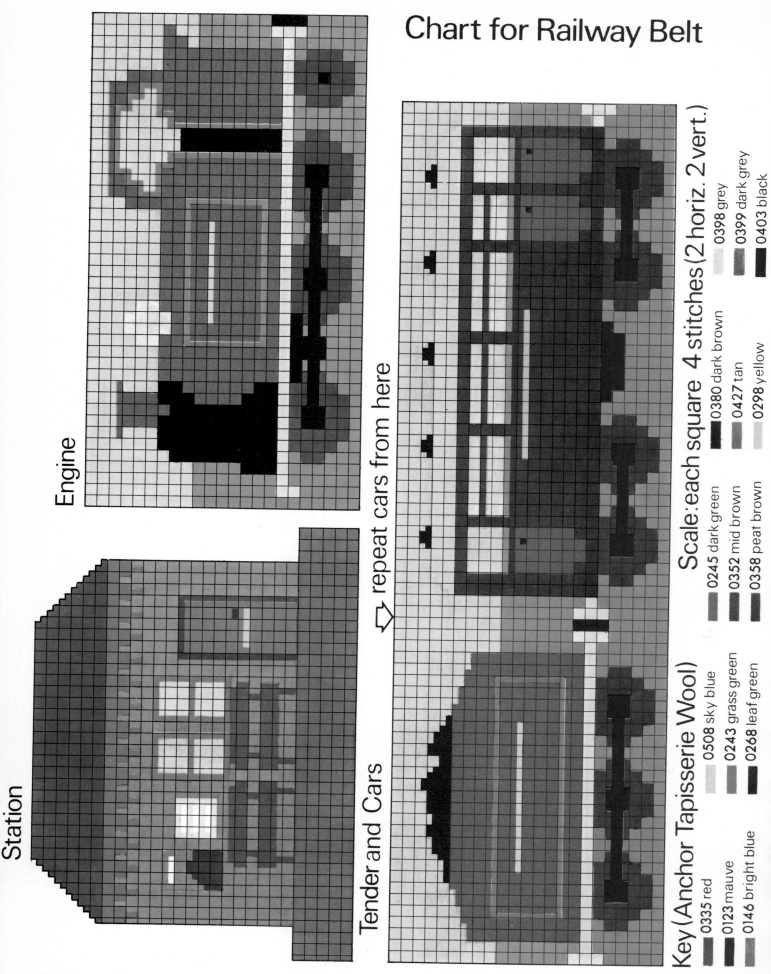

Chart for Railway Belt

Engine

Station

Tender and Cars

⇨ repeat cars from here

Scale: each square 4 stitches (2 horiz. 2 vert.)

Key (Anchor Tapisserie Wool)

0335 red
0123 mauve
0146 bright blue
0508 sky blue
0243 grass green
0268 leaf green
0245 dark green
0352 mid brown
0358 peat brown
0380 dark brown
0427 tan
0298 yellow
0398 grey
0399 dark grey
0403 black

66

Reflections on a frame

An unusual decorative idea for working a needlepoint border, is to frame a mirror or a picture with this highly original design in geometric patterns. Only three simple stitches are used to work the frame: tent stitch, petit point and flat or cushion stitch. The eye-catching effect is achieved by clever positioning of the stitches and interesting use of color.

Make the frame for either a stand-up mirror for your dressing table or a hanging mirror for your bedroom wall.

For the frame
6½ inches by 8½ inches

You will need
- ⅓ yard single thread canvas, 16 threads to the inch
- Anchor Tapisserie Wool in the following colors and quantities: 2 skeins 0403 black, 1 skein each of 0402 white, 0497 gray, 0432 blue, 0982 light brown, 0340 rust
- Piece of mirror glass measuring 6½ inches by 8½ inches
- Household cement
- Piece of stiff cardboard 6½ inches by 8½ inches
- Strong thread for lacing the canvas
- Piece of felt 6½ inches by 8½ inches for the backing

Method of working
The working chart indicates the stitches used and the direction in which they are worked. There are three different stitches used: tent stitch, petit point, and flat or cushion stitch. They are varied in direction to add interest to the design.

Use the illustration as a guide to placing the colors. The outer edge and the corners are worked in diagonal stripes of black and gray petit point. The zigzag border is worked in light brown, blue and rust. All the cushion stitch squares which form the inner border are worked in black and white, while the remaining squares of petit point are worked in black and white stripes. The tweed effect on the inside edge is achieved by working alternate black and white stitches.

NB Each corner and each long side of the frame is slightly different. The chart shows all four corners and part of the design on each side. To make the frame to the dimensions given, the design on each long side is repeated 6 times, and on each short side 4 times.

To trim the canvas
Trim the canvas around the frame leaving ¾ inch turnings. Cut out the center of the canvas, again leaving ¾ inch turnings. Make a diagonal cut at each inner corner, taking great care not to cut into the stitching. Fold back the inner turnings and stitch down.

To make up the mirror frame
Cut out a piece of cardboard the same size as the mirror glass and make slits in it as shown. Fold the flap back along the dotted line so that it juts out to form a stand for the mirror. Glue the cardboard to the back of the mirror.

Glue the frame to the front edge of the mirror, lining up the edges of the work with the edges of the glass. Turn the outer turnings to the back and, using strong thread, lace across the back of the mirror horizontally and vertically. On the horizontal lacing, make holes in the cardboard flap with the needle and pass the thread through so that the lacing lies flat.

Cut out a piece of felt the same size as the mirror for the backing. Make a vertical slit down the middle for the stand to emerge and then overcast the felt to the frame, making sure that no unworked canvas is left showing.

Or, to make a hanging mirror, omit the cardboard, and lace the canvas across the back of the mirror glass as before. Sew on a felt backing and attach two curtain rings to the top corners.

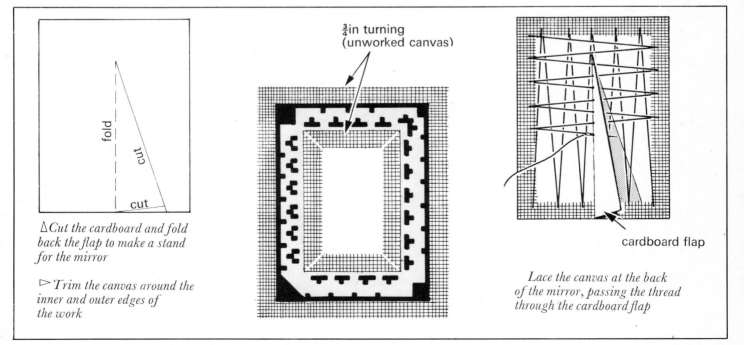

△ Cut the cardboard and fold back the flap to make a stand for the mirror

▷ Trim the canvas around the inner and outer edges of the work

¾ in turning (unworked canvas)

cardboard flap

Lace the canvas at the back of the mirror, passing the thread through the cardboard flap

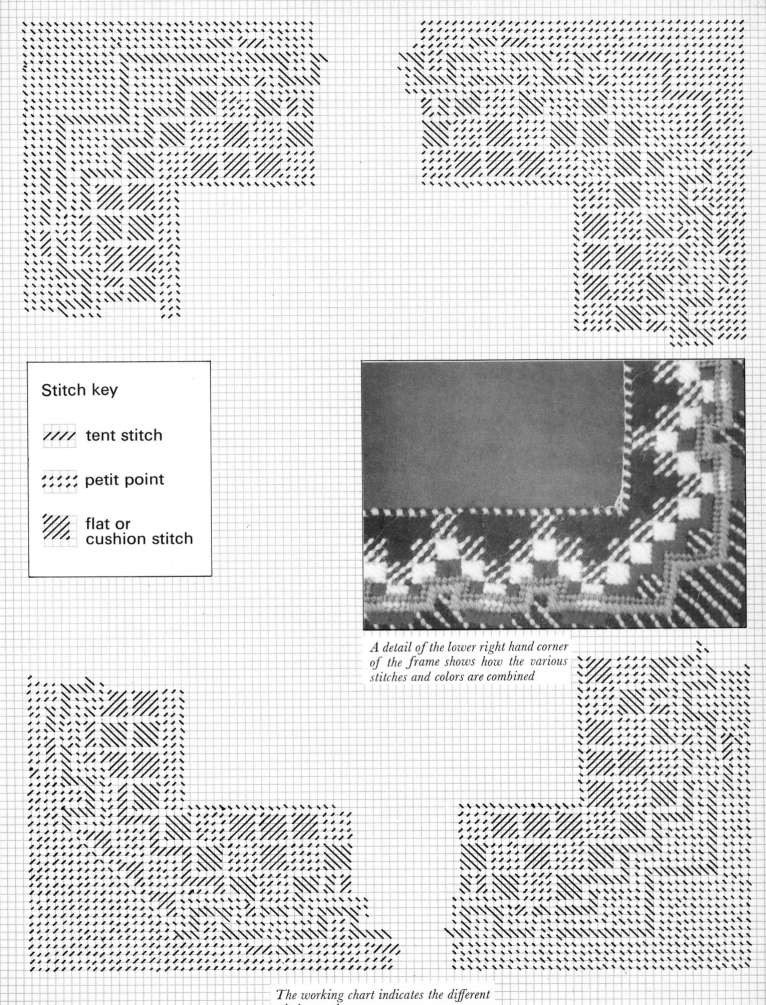

Stitch key

///// tent stitch

;;;;; petit point

///// flat or
cushion stitch

*A detail of the lower right hand corner
of the frame shows how the various
stitches and colors are combined*

*The working chart indicates the different
stitches used*

In the pink

You will need
- [ ] No 18 tapestry needle
- [ ] DMC Matania Embroidery in the following colors and quantities
- [ ] 12 skeins 2776 light old rose
- [ ] 7 skeins 2309 dark old rose

Make this beautiful belt to brighten up the simplest of garments. Team it up to the greatest effect with a tunic top, an evening caftan or a jumpsuit. Any color combination is suitable: shades of the same color or billiantly contrasting ones, perhaps chosen to wear with a specific garment.

For the belt
¼ yard 27 inches or 1 yard 23 inches (depending on the waist size) single thread canvas (16 threads to the inch)

Method of working
The design can be extended in length to fit any waist measurement.

To give the most attractive results the entire design should be worked, although a simpler alternative is just to work the central motif, then fill in the remaining area in a single color.

The design is worked in satin stitch, using DMC Matania. The tracing pattern indicates the position of each color in the design.

Transferring the design
Place the tracing pattern under the canvas and trace the design and the outline of the belt onto the canvas with an indelible marking pen or acrylic paints in a neutral color. If desired, fill in the design with acrylic paints, using somewhat more subdued colors than those for the yarns to be used for working the design.

The design is repeated as a mirror image where indicated. Repeat as much of the secondary motif along the narrow portion of the belt as is required: a repeat of 1-1½ times on each side should be adequate. Allow at least 1 inch at each end for turnings when making up.

Trace pattern for belt embroidery
Repeat this motif
as required
to accommodate
waist measurement

Signs of
the times

We don't claim to be able to predict your future—but we can help you to make your own sign of the zodiac in needlepoint for personal accessories such as belts, pockets, handbags or jewelery. Zodiac signs might be lucky for the family too—what about a set of table mats and matching napkins, each decorated with the owner's own sign?

The signs in this chapter are for those born between March 21st and September 22nd and the remainder of the signs for Libra to Pisces appear in the next chapter. Simple designs such as these are intended to inspire you: don't just accept a design as being a certain size or for a certain purpose. Use them smaller—or much larger. Group several small signs together or use a single sign, very large for a wall panel. Consider the designs as a stepping-off place to create all kinds of new designs by using contrasting yarns, contrasting textures and stitches. Use your creativity and make simple charted designs part of your personal design library.

Shading with tent stitch
After experimenting with some of the rich, textured stitches you might perhaps feel that tent stitch is not so adventurous. But this stitch really comes into its own with shading. Each of the Zodiac signs is an example of how a three-dimensional effect can be built up with a limited pattern of closely related colors.

Use yarn in the same way that an artist uses his paints: darker tones for shaded areas, paler tones for highlights. Or some of the signs would look extremely effective worked in one color or with metallic yarn on a contrasting color background.

Large or small
The motifs can be worked to different sizes by using fine or coarse canvas. For instance for a tiny motif, work on single weave canvas with 24 threads to 1 inch, using crewel wool, 6-strand floss or pure silk. Using this mesh, the finished signs will measure about $1\frac{1}{8}$ inch by $1\frac{3}{8}$ inch, an ideal size for mounting as a brooch or pendant. Worked on double weave canvas with 10 double threads to 1 inch using crewel wool, tapestry yarn, or 6-strand floss, the signs will measure $2\frac{7}{8}$ inches by $3\frac{1}{4}$ inches. On coarse canvas, metallic yarns in gold or silver can also be incorporated into the design.

Suggestions for use
Worked on fine mesh canvas, the motifs would make unusual gifts in pendants, brooches or a set of buttons. Or several motifs of one sign joined together would make a belt, or a miniature wall panel would look quite charming worked in all twelve designs.

You could work the larger motifs three in a row to fit under a transparent door fingerplate or work twelve separate squares to make a pillow, a compact case, purse or glasses case.

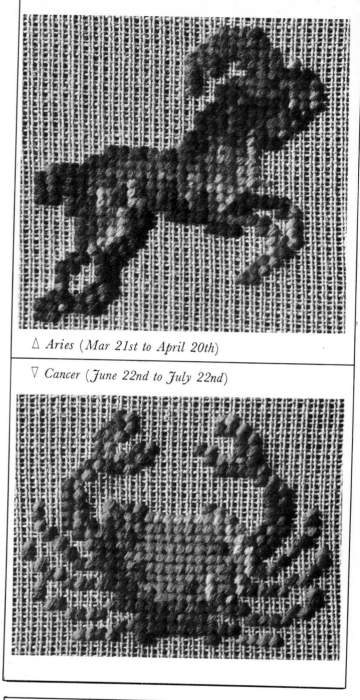

△ *Aries (Mar 21st to April 20th)*

▽ *Cancer (June 22nd to July 22nd)*

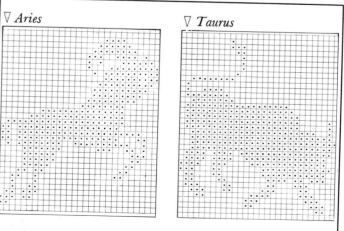

▽ *Aries*   ▽ *Taurus*

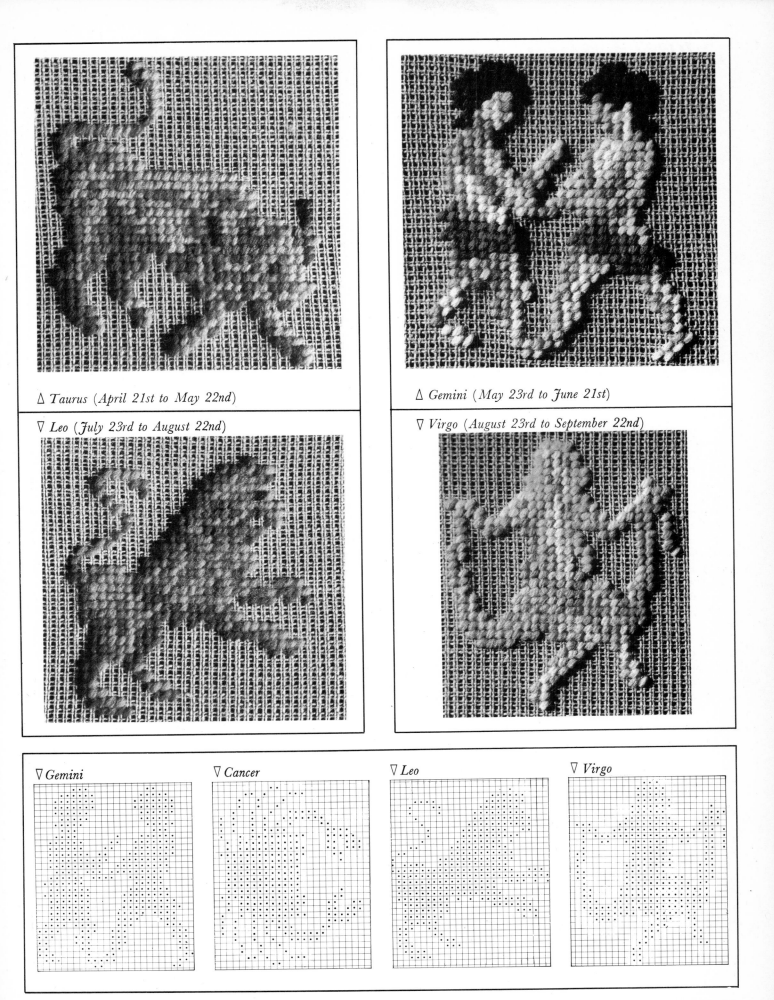

△ *Taurus (April 21st to May 22nd)*

△ *Gemini (May 23rd to June 21st)*

▽ *Leo (July 23rd to August 22nd)*

▽ *Virgo (August 23rd to September 22nd)*

▽ *Gemini*

▽ *Cancer*

▽ *Leo*

▽ *Virgo*

From Libra to Pisces

Here are the signs covering the months from September to March—Libra, Scorpio, Sagittarius, Capricorn, Aquarius and Pisces. Work the signs on fine canvas as suggested or, by following the instructions below, enlarge the designs.

With coarser canvas, using a greater variety of stitches and yarns, exciting effects can be achieved.

To enlarge a design

You will need
- Graph paper
- A sharp, soft pencil

You can vary the size of a needlepoint design by working on different weights of canvas: the coarser the canvas, the larger the design. The following instructions can be adapted to enlarge almost any uncomplicated design.

Shade in with pencil four squares of the graph paper for each square on the original chart. Each of the large, penciled squares is then used for either 4 tent stitches or 1 square stitch. This enlarged design can now be worked on single weave canvas, giving scope for a larger variety of stitches such as cushion stitch, rice stitch, double cross-stitch or long-legged stitch, used either for the motif or the background. For instance, try the effect of the motif in rice stitch with the background in cushion stitch or long-legged cross-stitch. Have fun experimenting with different textures—it is surprising how different a design can look worked in a combination of stitches.

The single enlarged design can be used as a central motif on a pillow, bag or footstool top. A panel made up of all twelve motifs would look striking, particularly if worked as a sampler, each motif in a different combination of stitches and threads.

NB Sagittarius: To work the strings on the bow in this motif, stitch the background first and then work 2 long stitches for the strings. If you are working the motif on an article which will get hard wear, catch the long threads with invisible nylon yarn.

For luck, work your sign of the zodiac for a glamorous belt buckle

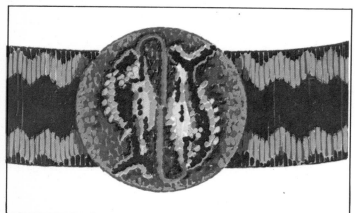

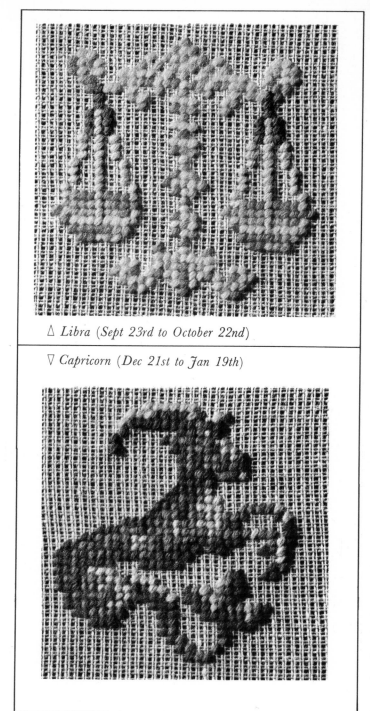

△ *Libra (Sept 23rd to October 22nd)*

▽ *Capricorn (Dec 21st to Jan 19th)*

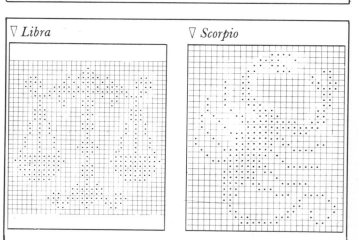

▽ *Libra*   ▽ *Scorpio*

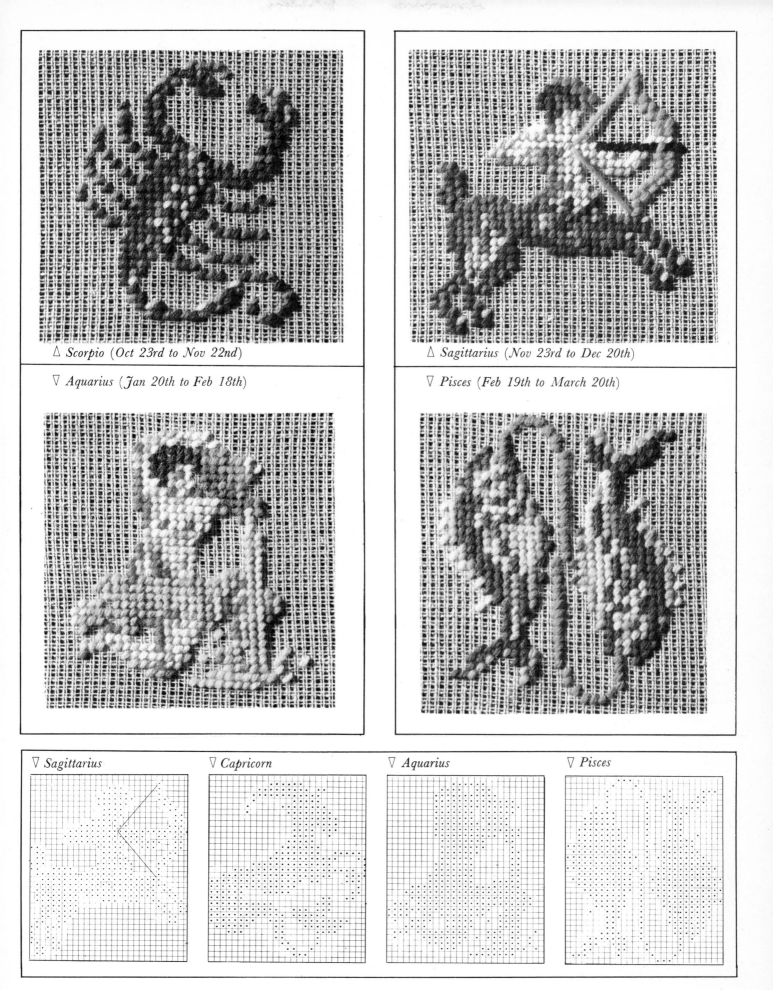

△ *Scorpio (Oct 23rd to Nov 22nd)*

△ *Sagittarius (Nov 23rd to Dec 20th)*

▽ *Aquarius (Jan 20th to Feb 18th)*

▽ *Pisces (Feb 19th to March 20th)*

▽ *Sagittarius*

▽ *Capricorn*

▽ *Aquarius*

▽ *Pisces*

It's a frame up

All the colors of the rainbow are worked into this eye-catching needlepoint picture frame. Using only 3 simple stitches, the frame would make an ideal project for a beginner, although the most experienced needle-woman would enjoy working such a variety of colors. We chose an arrangement of pressed spring flowers to echo the frame's bright colors, but it would look equally good surrounding a mirror or any favorite picture.

For the frame
12 inches square

You will need
- ☐ ½ yard single thread canvas, 16 threads to the inch
- ☐ Anchor Tapisserie Wool in the following colors and quantities: 4 skeins 0162 blue, 3 skeins 013 red, 2 skeins each 0239 green, 0295 yellow, 0314 orange, 0106 purple; 1 skein 096 mauve
- ☐ Piece of glass measuring 12 inches square
- ☐ Household cement
- ☐ Piece of stiff cardboard 12 inches square
- ☐ Piece of felt 12 inches square for backing
- ☐ Strong thread for lacing the canvas
- ☐ Two small curtain rings

Method of working
The working chart shows the stitches used and the direction in which they are placed. Only 3 stitches are used: tent stitch, petit point and flat or cushion stitch. The variety of colors and the direction in which the stitches are worked add interest and texture.

Use the photograph as a guide to placing the colors. Diagonal stripes of petit point around the inner and outer edges add a pretty beading effect to the frame. When working the corners, make sure to follow the chart carefully as all the petit point squares are worked in different directions.

NB The center stitches of the top and bottom are arranged slightly differently from those at the sides, as is shown on the chart.

To trim the canvas
Trim the canvas around the frame leaving ¾ inch turnings. Cut out the center of the canvas, again leaving ¾ inch turnings. Make a diagonal cut at each inner corner, taking great care not to cut into the stitching. Fold back the inner turnings and stitch down.

To make up the picture frame
Cut out a piece of cardboard the same size as the frame. Place your picture over the cardboard and the piece of glass over the picture. Glue the frame to the edge of the glass, lining up the outer edges of the work with the edges of the glass. Turn the outer turnings to the back and, with strong thread, lace across the back of the picture horizontally and vertically.

Cut out a piece of felt the same size as the picture for the backing and overcast to the frame. Sew the two curtain rings to the felt and loop a piece of cord through the rings.

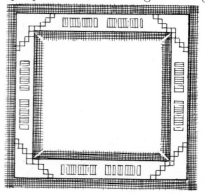

Trim the canvas around the inner and outer edges of the work, leaving a ¾ inch turning of unworked canvas

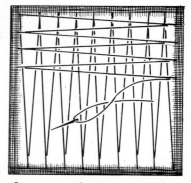

Lace across the canvas at the back of the picture

Stitch chart for frame

A detail of one corner of the frame shows how the colors and stitches are combined

Stitch key

 tent stitch

 flat or cushion stitch

 petit point

The working chart indicates the different stitches used and the direction in which they are worked

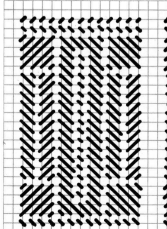

center of side

77

Needlepoint pockets

Abstract flower shapes worked on a checkerboard background make these smart pockets for a jersey coatdress. Jackets, vests and jeans can all be brightened up by the addition of one or more of these pockets, worked in attractive subtle shades.

For two pockets
each measuring 4½ inches by 5 inches

You will need

☐ ¼ yard single thread canvas, 16 threads to the inch
☐ Anchor Tapisserie Wool in the following quantities and colors: 2 skeins each 0504 light gray, 0497 blue gray, 0498 rose beige; 1 skein each 0388 gold, 0392 beige, 0438 gray green, 0428 rust, 0982 gray, 0380 dark brown, 0399 pewter, 0871 plum.

Adapt the size of the design for various uses

Method of working

Follow the working chart given for one of the pockets; then work the other pocket as a mirror image of this design. As the design is asymmetrical, the two pockets are thus evenly balanced.

The key to the working chart indicates colors and stitches to be used in the design. Tent stitch, petit point and flat or cushion stitch are the only stitches required and the varying direction of some stitches adds interest to the design.

Adjusting the design

In order to increase or decrease the dimensions of the pockets, substitute canvas with a smaller or larger grid. The size and shape of the design can also be adjusted by altering the number of stitches in the border. Make whatever color changes or substitutions are required to co-ordinate the pockets with a particular garment.

Alternative uses

To make a pincushion, decorative box top, mirror back or cover for an address book, work the design on single thread canvas with 18 threads to the inch.

Or work four or more panels and sew them together to make a stool cover, perhaps trimming it with braid or cord to match the stitched border. As before, alter the border area to achieve the size required.

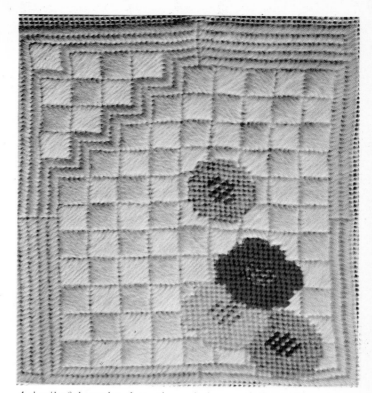

A detail of the pocket shows the worked canvas before making up

Key

Background:	light gray 0504
	blue gray 0497
Border:	rose beige 0498
	light gray 0504
	gold 0388
	beige 0392
Flowers:	gray green 0438
	gold 0388
	rust 0428
	gray 0982
Flower centers:	dark brown 0380
	pewter 0399
	plum 0871
	gray green 0438
Stitches:	Tent stitch
	Petit point
	Flat or cushion stitch

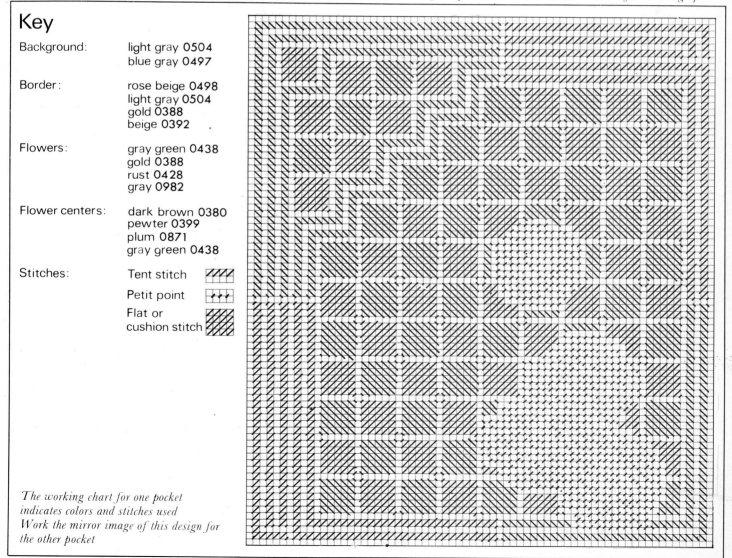

*The working chart for one pocket indicates colors and stitches used
Work the mirror image of this design for the other pocket*

A Danish rose

Cross-stitch is one of the oldest forms of embroidery. For centuries it has been used in traditional European folk and peasant embroideries to decorate national costumes and household articles. Each country has developed its own particular style to such an extent that it is possible to determine where a particular piece of work or design originated. For instance, modern Danish cross-stitch designs usually depict forms in a very realistic manner. The rounded shapes of flowers, birds and animals are embroidered in delicate pretty colors in carefully selected tones which, when worked together, enhance this realistic effect. This delightful rose motif is typical of the Danish style in cross-stitch, and can be used in many exciting ways. Here it is shown worked in two ways to create completely contrasting effects. One rose is worked in chunky yarns on canvas, the other in stranded floss on fine linen and mounted in a tiny gold frame. To work a traditional design is sometimes a welcome change.

Worked on linen with 24 threads to 1 inch over 2 threads each way, the rose will measure about 2½ inches by 2½ inches.

Worked as a pillow the same motif measures about 7½ inches by 7½ inches—the different scale is achieved by working the cross-stitch over 3 threads each way on single weave canvas with 12 threads to 1 inch using 2 strands of knitting worsted throughout.

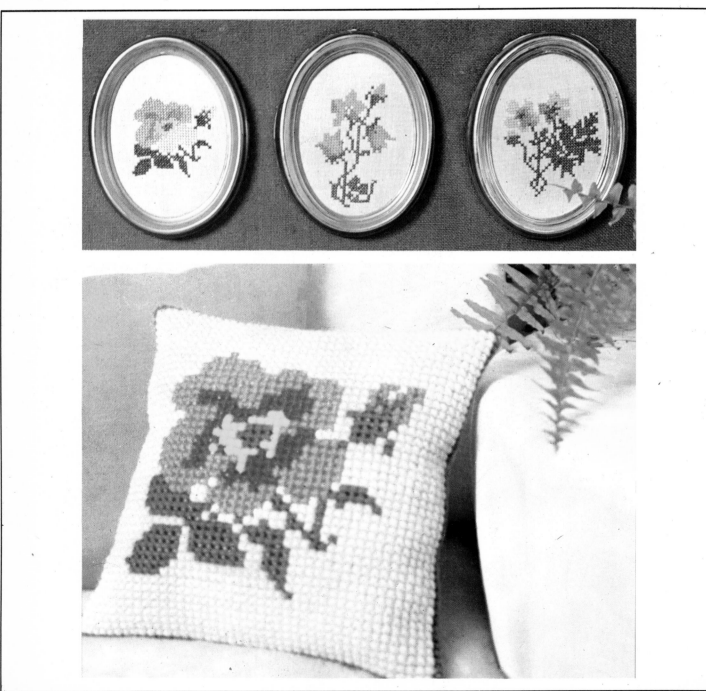

Bolero to match all moods

Make this beautiful bolero to suit every occasion. Wear it with a flowing gipsy skirt and blouse for a romantic mood. Transform a classic camel turtle neck sweater and pants into a striking outfit, or add a touch of spice to a plain long-sleeved day dress in a toning color. The bolero is straightforward to make and is worked in gros point stitch.

For the bolero
To fit 34 inch to 36 inch bust

You will need
- [ ] Anchor Tapisserie Wool in the following colors and quantities: 6 skeins 0429 pink; 5 skeins each of 0388 ecru, 0873 plum; 4 skeins each of 028 carnation, 0402 white; 3 skeins 0577 cyclamen
- [ ] $1\frac{3}{8}$ yards double thread canvas, 19 inches wide, 10 holes to the inch
- [ ] $1\frac{1}{4}$ yards matching lining fabric 36 inches wide $\frac{3}{4}$ yard matching light woolen fabric 36 inches wide for back of bolero
- [ ] $3\frac{1}{2}$ yards matching braid, 1 inch wide
- [ ] Tapestry frame with 23 inch tapes
- [ ] One tapestry needle No 18

Working trammed gros point stitch
The design is worked throughout in trammed gros point stitch as shown in the diagrams. In diagram 1, work a trammed stitch from left to right, then pull the needle through and insert again up and over the crossed threads. In diagram 2, pull the needle through on the lower line two double threads (vertical) to the left in readiness for the next stitch.

As the canvas is tightly stretched on a frame, you will need to use both hands for working. With the right hand on top of the canvas, insert the needle downward through the canvas, pulling it through with the left hand. With the left hand, push the needle upward through the canvas, pulling it out with the right hand.

Method of working
Cut two pieces from the canvas, each measuring $24\frac{3}{4}$ inches by 19 inches and mark the center of each piece both horizontally and vertically with a line of basting stitches. Mount the first piece of canvas in the frame with the raw edges to the tapes.

The chart gives the complete left front of the bolero, indicating the areas of different colors. The central lines are indicated by arrows which should coincide with the basting stitches. Each background square on the chart represents the double thread of the canvas.

Commence the design centrally and work following the chart, using the letter and sign key to place the colors. To work the right side, mount the second piece of canvas in the frame and repeat the design in reverse.

Blocking the canvas and cutting out
The canvas may require blocking when removed from the frame. Dampen the canvas, then pin it to a clean dry board pulling it gently to the correct shape. Leave to dry naturally.

Trim around the canvas except for the dart, leaving $\frac{5}{8}$ inch turnings on the shoulder and side seams. Trim as close to all the other edges as possible, taking care not to cut into the stitching. Make the pattern for the back of the bolero, enlarging from the layout diagram onto squared paper, and cut out the woolen fabric and the lining. Cut the lining for the two front pieces using the worked canvas plus the unworked borders as a guide.

Stitch the darts on the bolero fronts, either by machine or using a firm back stitch. Slash up the center of the darts and press open with a slightly damp cloth and a medium hot iron. Stitch the darts on the back of the bolero and join the canvas and the woolen fabric at the side and shoulder seams. Press seams open. Stitch the lining in the same way, then place the bolero and the lining together wrong sides facing. Baste around the edge of the bolero and around the armholes, matching seams. Machine stitch $\frac{1}{4}$ inch in from all the edges.

Edge the bolero with braid as follows. Turn under $\frac{5}{8}$ inch at one end of the braid and start pinning it to the right side of the bolero from a side seam, folding it so that half shows on the right side and half on the wrong side. Pin all around the edges of the bolero and the armholes, then make the end neat by again turning it under $\frac{5}{8}$ inch and stitching it to join at the seam. Stitch the braid on the right side, and to the lining using a small slip stitch.

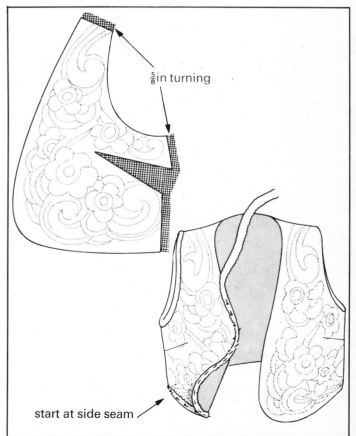

$\frac{5}{8}$ in turning

start at side seam

Trim around the canvas except for the dart, leaving $\frac{5}{8}$ inch seam allowance on the shoulder and side seams
Pin the braid to the right side of the bolero, folding it under so that half shows on the right side and half on the wrong side

Graph pattern for Back

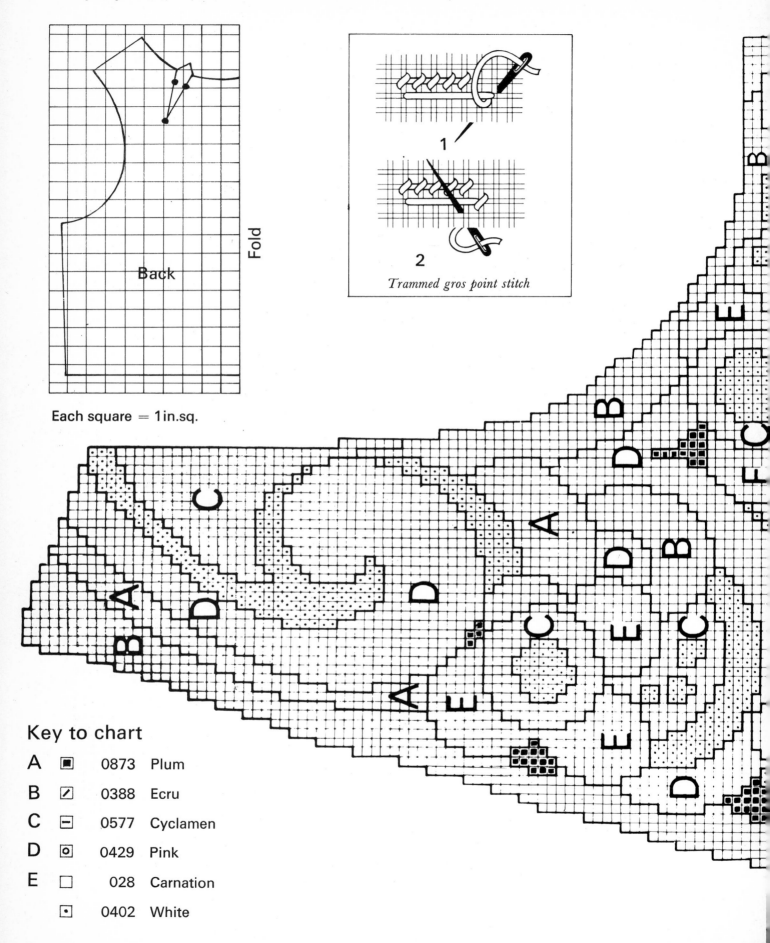

Back

Fold

Each square = 1 in. sq.

Trammed gros point stitch

Key to chart

A	■	0873	Plum
B	☑	0388	Ecru
C	⊟	0577	Cyclamen
D	⊙	0429	Pink
E	□	028	Carnation
	⊡	0402	White

Working chart for left front of Bolero
Reverse for right front

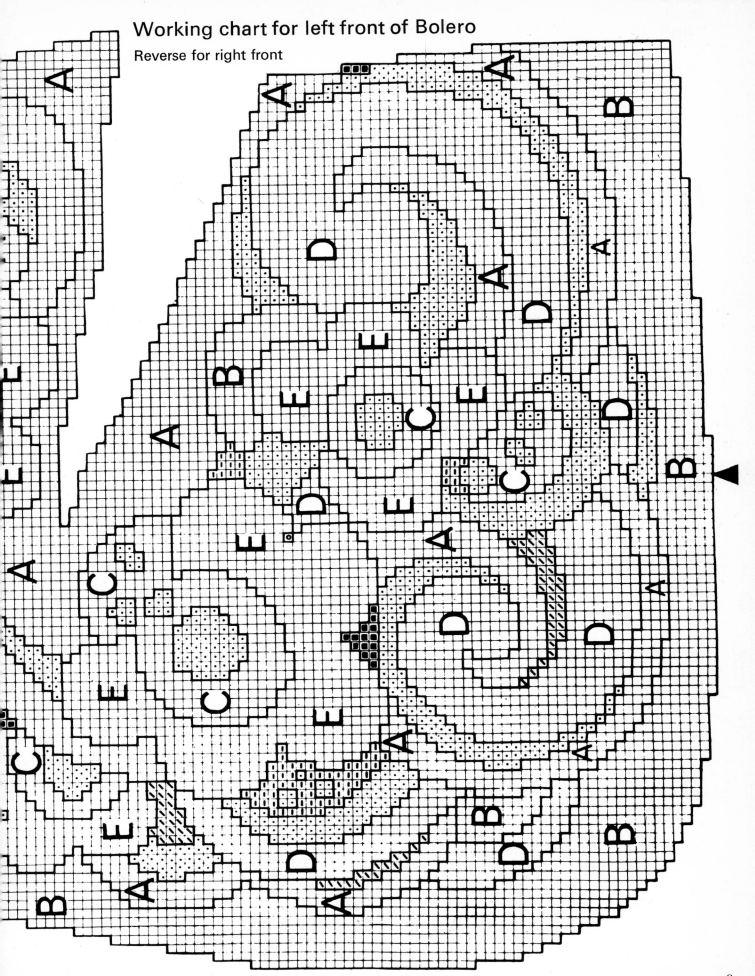

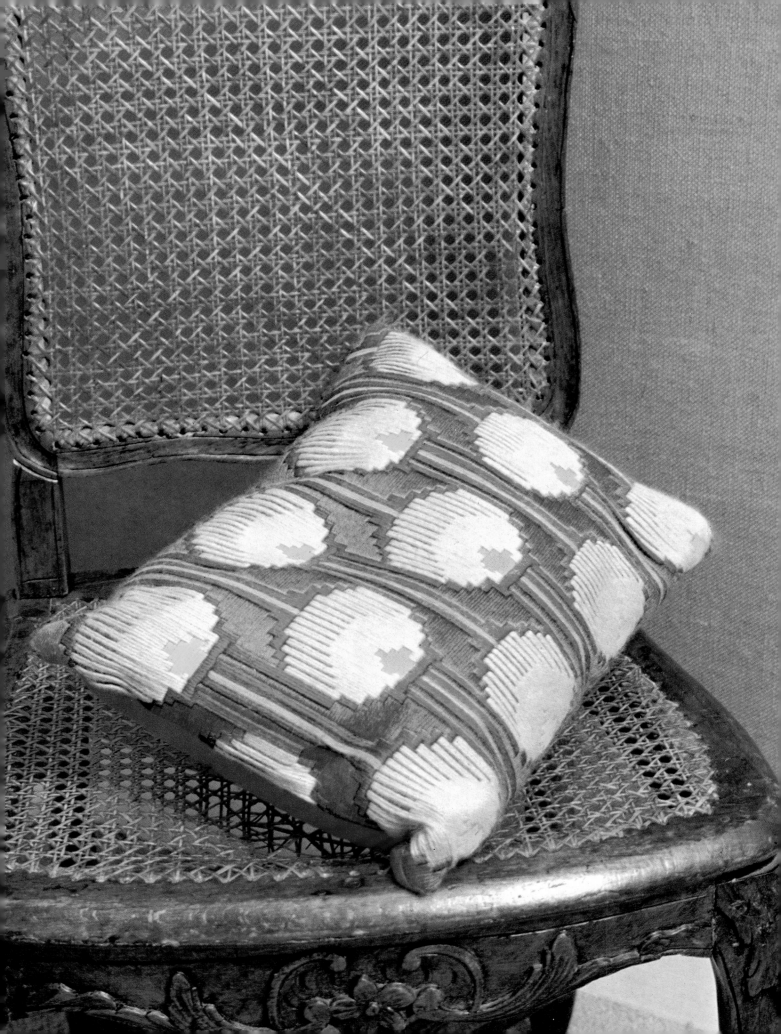

Art Deco pillow

"Lamp stands" is a bold design for a needlepoint pillow. Work the entire design in horizontal and vertical rows of satin stitch.

For the pillow
16¾ inches by 11¾ inches

You will need
☐ ½ yard single thread canvas, 16 holes to the inch

☐ DMC Tapestry Wool, Article 482 in the following quantities and colors:
6 skeins 7501 beige; 2 skeins 7435 yellow; 6 skeins 7146 salmon; 7 skeins 7317 blue
☐ Pillow form or Dacron wadding
☐ Fabric in toning color for backing

Method of working
Following the working chart for the design, use the stitches and colors designated in the key. The chart gives one half the design to be worked; repeat as a mirror image where indicated.

Alternative colors
In order to complement another color scheme with the pillow, substitute these shades in DMC Tapestry Wool: 7351 pale green, 7436 gold, 7363 olive green and 7307 dark blue.

The working chart for the color scheme illustrated is shown overleaf and the alternative color scheme is shown below, or you can choose a color scheme of your own

Key to working chart

☐ **7501** beige
vertical satin stitch

7146 salmon
horizontal satin stitch

7317 blue
vertical satin stitch

7435 yellow
horizontal satin stitch
(strips between bulbs – vertical satin stitch)

Key to alternative color chart

7363 olive green

7307 dark blue

7351 pale green

7436 gold

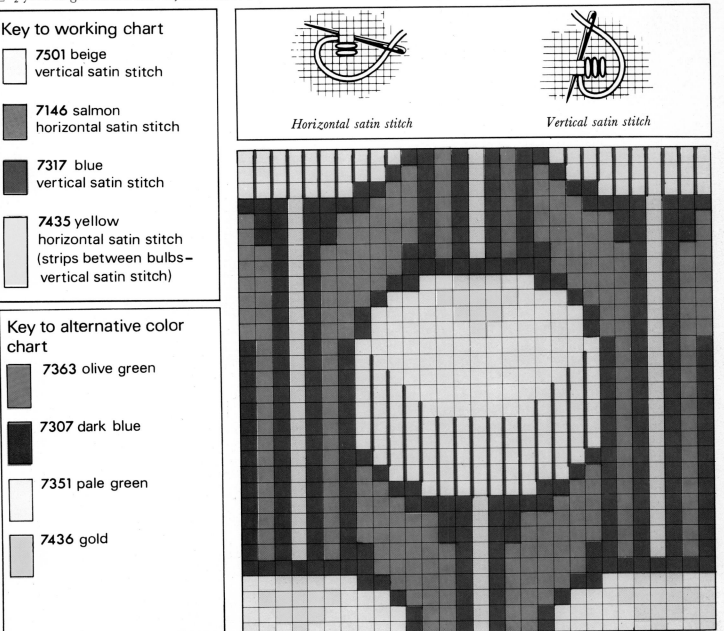

Horizontal satin stitch   *Vertical satin stitch*

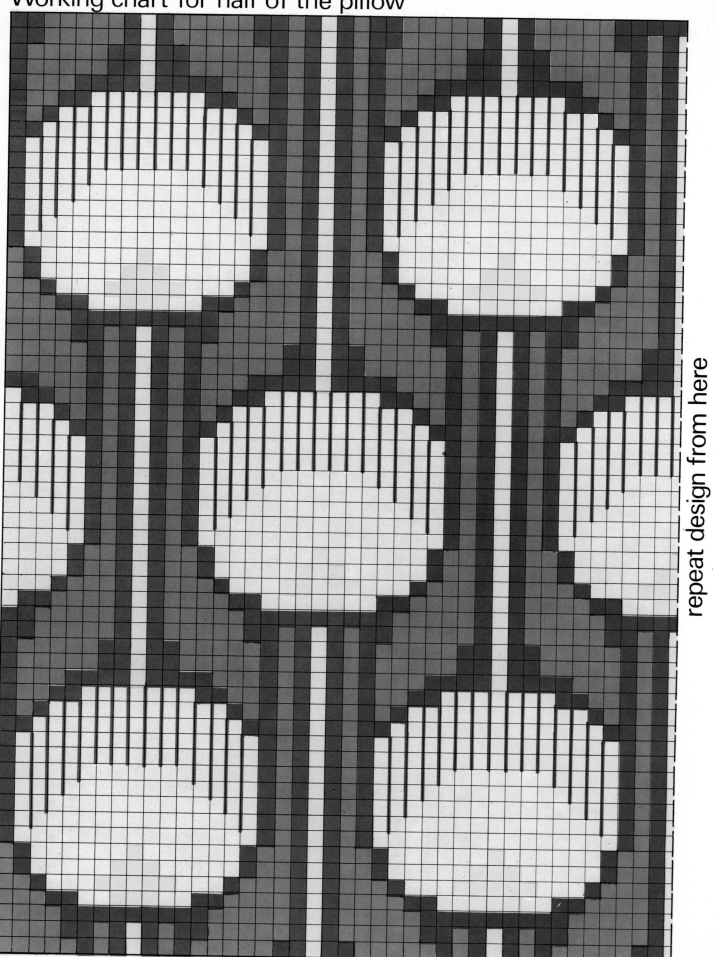

repeat design from here